dealing with your anger

For my sons James, David, and Frank

ordering

Trade bookstores in the U.S. and Canada please contact:

Publishers Group West
1700 Fourth Street, Berkeley CA 94710
Phone: (800) 788-3123   Fax: (800) 351-5073

Hunter House books are available at bulk discounts for textbook course adoptions; to qualifying community, health-care, and government organizations; and for special promotions and fund-raising. For details please contact:

Special Sales Department
Hunter House Inc., PO Box 2914
Alameda CA 94501-0914
Phone: (510) 865-5282   Fax: (510) 865-4295
E-mail: ordering@hunterhouse.com

Individuals can order our books from most bookstores, by calling **(800) 266-5592**, or from our website at **www.hunterhouse.com**

dealing with your anger

---

self-help solutions for men

Frank Donovan, MAASW

First published in 1999 in Australia and New Zealand by
Finch Publishing Pty Limited, ACN 057 285 248, PO Box 120,
Lane Cove, NSW 1595, Australia.

Hunter House Inc., Publishers
PO Box 2914
Alameda CA 94501-0914

Library of Congress Cataloging-in-Publication Data

Donovan, Frank.
　　Dealing with your anger : self-help solutions for men / Frank
Donovan.—1st ed.
　　　　p. cm.
　　Includes bibliographical references and index.
　　ISBN-13: 978-0-89793-344-5 — ISBN-10: 0-89793-344-3
1. Anger. I. Title.

BF575.A5 D66 2001
152.4'7'081—dc21　　　　　　　　　　　　　　2001026472

Project Credits

Illustrations: Phil Somerville
Cover Design: Brian Dittmar
Book Design and Production:
　Jinni Fontana
Copy Editor: Kelley Blewster
Proofreader: John David Marion
Indexer: Kathy Talley-Jones
Acquisitions Editor: Jeanne Brondino
Associate Editor: Alexandra Mummery
Editorial and Production Assistant:
　Emily Tryer

Sales and Marketing Assistant:
　Earlita K. Chenault
Publicity Manager: Sara Long
Customer Service Manager:
　Christina Sverdrup
Order Fulfillment: Lakdhon Lama
Administrator: Theresa Nelson
Computer Support: Peter Eichelberger
Publisher: Kiran S. Rana

Manufactured in the United States of America

9 8 7 6 5 4 3 2　　　First Edition　　　12 13 14 15 16

contents

caution: a note for men in crisis

If you have come to this book still angry from a serious, abusive, or violent episode of anger with your girlfriend, partner, or wife, do one of these two things right now:

1. For the fit and able: Go for a run or fast walk until you have exhausted yourself physically. Do it now; then come back and read the table titled "Men's Safety Check," on the next page.

2. For the less fit and able: Sit back, close your eyes, rest your hands open with arms unfolded, and take ten deep breaths like this:

   Breathe in deeply down to your diaphragm.

   Hold each breath in for the count of three seconds.

   Breathe out until you empty your lungs right down to your diaphragm. On each breath out, let physical tension flow out of your body through your limbs. Start with your head and work downwards with each breath out until you have relaxed your whole body.

Do this relaxation now; then come back and read the table titled "Men's Safety Check," on the next page.

what you should do now

If you have answered either *yes* or *maybe* to any one of the questions in the Men's Safety Check, you have a responsibility to guarantee the safety of your partner and any children at risk. The best and fairest way to do that is to move out of your home, or not be with your partner, while you work on your anger and make yourself safe to be with.

men's safety check

questions	answers
	Check *yes, maybe,* or *no* for each question.
Have you ever hit, kicked, thrown, or used physical force on or against anyone who has ever lived with you or who has been in an intimate relationship with you— whether angry or not?	☐ Yes ☐ Maybe ☐ No
Do you suspect that anyone with whom you currently live (including children), or with whom you have an intimate relation- ship, has ever been scared of your anger or violence or might be so right now?	☐ Yes ☐ Maybe ☐ No
Look at yourself squarely in a mirror and ask yourself, "Is there a risk that I could harm or scare my present partner or children in my anger—even if I would never mean to?"	☐ Yes ☐ Maybe ☐ No

Anything will do: a motel room, your buddy's place, your parents' or a relative's home, a rooming house, hostel, cabin, caravan, or trailer park—any of these that you can afford, and where you can be reached by your wife, partner, or children. It is not permanent; it might only be for a few weeks. Unless one or both of you decide to separate, you will get back together— just as soon as you can guarantee your partner and children that you are safe to be with.

In some cases the man's partner and children have moved out instead; not only is this unfair to her and disruptive for children (who are already feeling unsafe), it fails to put the responsibility where it belongs—with the man whose anger or violence is the problem!

Many men before you have moved out until they solved their problems; most moved back home later when it was safe to do so. Believe them when they say, "Some inconvenience now is a small price to pay for a better life later, one in which the women and children around you feel safe and free from fear."

— Frank Donovan
July 2001

important note

The material in this book is intended to provide a guide for men dealing with issues of anger. Every effort has been made to provide accurate and dependable information, and the contents of this book have been compiled in consultation with other professionals. However, the reader should be aware that professionals in the field may have differing opinions, and legal policies may differ from state to state and are changing constantly. The publisher, authors, and editors cannot be held responsible for any error, omission, professional disagreement, or dated material.

The ideas, procedures, and suggestions contained in this book are designed to encourage men to work through their anger, but are not intended to replace a professional program. If you have any questions or concerns about applying this information, please consult an anger-management program or a licensed therapist. The author and publisher assume no responsibility for any outcome of the use of these materials individually or in consultation with a professional or group.

foreword

"How do I deal with my anger?" To have arrived at this question, I will as a man have had to realize, or feel, or have just been told that my expressions of this emotion have become unmanageable, frightening, or hurtful. I may have had to face my capacity to hurt or intimidate another or do harm to myself. Probably I will have had to face the fact of having hurt another. And if that has happened, then more likely than not the one I hurt will have been the one easiest for me to hurt: my partner or lover or child.

What does it mean, in any of the above contexts, for me to deal with my anger? At the very least, I will have to recognize my anger as a feeling. And to face that I have feelings, against my probably learned habit of not noticing, or suppressing, or controlling them. To face the probable lack of a vocabulary to talk about them. To identify feelings behind the anger. And perhaps, to face a fear of dealing with them.

If I've hurt someone, I'll have to look at why I made that person my target. If that person is a man, what does this say about how I've learned to interact with men in the case of conflict? If a child, what might this mean about what I have learned to pass on, generation to generation? If myself, what could this signify about how I've learned to treat myself? And finally, if that person is a woman, I will have to look at what I've done against the much broader backdrop of the facts about violence men do to women—the daily facts of discrimination, harassment, and abuse, the sum of which are almost impossible for me to hold before my mind. How does my action fit here? What attitudes about women might it disclose? Where do these attitudes come from?

I'll have to begin to consider what my life has been about as a man. What I've been told about how I was supposed to act, how I was supposed to deal with feelings, and how I was supposed to use anger. What was I told? What was done to me to make sure I learned this lesson? What was done to my feelings? How might I have been conditioned physically to be tough physically or to hide my feelings altogether?

Finally, I'll have to ask for help; to expect to go through a process; and to expect that ultimately the process will be an ongoing, lifelong one.

In other words, to deal with anger I will have to stop "acting like a man" and, in the best sense of the words, I'll have to be a real man.

Dealing with Your Anger is a self-help book on how to handle anger, predominantly for men with special attention to men who turn their anger to violence. It reads straightforwardly, chapter to chapter, and avowedly follows a process parallel to a therapeutic one. Frank Donovan, a practicing therapist in Australia who has worked with men on these issues for many years, takes from the very beginning an engaging man-to-man approach, by turns serious and light, right from his opening line, "I am an angry man." On a subject patently loaded with possibilities for guilt, gloom, remorse, denial, self-hate, or just general "male" dourness he manages to stay conversational, light, but face-to-face. He addresses us directly. He speaks openly of his own bouts with anger and violence when deployed with Australian forces in Vietnam during the U.S-Vietnamese conflict, and later when running for political office. Finally, he laces his writing throughout with stories and statements from the men with whom he has worked.

Donovan uses clarifying, sometimes funny, stereotypically "male" images to help his readers cope with exercises: the toolshed as a place of sanity, the power saw as a tool like anger, building a raft as a process for gathering alternatives, traffic light approaches to gauging anger, and firefighting as a strategy for thinking about handling anger. The book is additionally accessible with its brief chapters, forms to fill out, directions to the reader to get started with new processes or review or re-do earlier ones, and its beginning-to-end graded exercises.

The exercises in fact are the heart of *Dealing with Your Anger*. To deal with anger means to work at it: the BioScan, Personal Anger Monitor, traffic-light model, and other tools Donovan offers are to be used, evaluated, and used again. Behind them lies the author's conviction that male anger and violence are intimately connected to male socialization, are even an assault upon selfhood. To address something this basic requires a process with cycles and stages—and work.

Donovan has extensively revised his work, originally published in Australia, for publication in the United States. There aren't many books here in the self-help anger-management market. There are publications dealing with counseling for abusive men, curricula, and group manuals. Against the latter, Donovan's book is bracing, personable, accessible. There is a standing need for books helping men to deal with anger. There is always a need for new books to help men recognize and stop abuse. Therapists for men who are otherwise uncertain about anger issues might usefully assign the book. And then there's just a need for self-help books for men in general that pay attention to emotional well-being. *Dealing with Your Anger* will be a valuable aid in each of these contexts.

A word of caution. In the United States, the battered women's movement in particular has brought one major outcome of men's violence associated with anger—the battering of partners and children—to public notice. Battering has received institutional definition in legal and medical realms: hundreds of programs around the country now offer "batterer intervention" and "anger management" for men and sometimes women. They range from short-term behavior-management groups to long-term "treatment" and therapy. Participants are clients who may refer themselves or be sent by the courts. There is ongoing debate about which approaches "work" and whether any do, given the much larger context of male socialization and gender inequality implied by so much violence. And whether they work or not, it is estimated that only one in ten men who are facing these issues actually make it to such programs.

Any man who is considering dealing with anger must answer the question about whether violence is involved, even or especially where the dividing line between anger and violence is unclear. Moreover, if as a man I examine my own angry behavior, I may not be in the best position to judge whether violence is involved. And, where there is the fact or threat of violence, *Dealing with Your Anger* will not be enough. Part of the power of Donovan's work are his statements, from the beginning, that anger is especially a men's problem, and that while anger is important for men to explore and confront, not bury, it must be distinguished and separated from violence. On the opening page the reader must assess if he is in a violent situation right now. In several places in the text, Donovan warns readers who are dealing with violence that they must obtain help beyond the book. Not to acknowledge the danger and risk they represent to others is at once to fail in the work. Only when I as a man dealing with violence begin to get that help from both this book and from sources outside of this book, will I really be "dealing."

The United States edition of *Dealing with Your Anger* comes into print in the weeks following the explosive destruction of the World Trade Center in New York. It explicitly relates its issues to highly publicized acts of violence, from the Port Arthur massacres in Australia to the shooting at Columbine High School and the bombing in Oklahoma City in the United States. In these contexts of rage and loss, a book dealing with anger has a renewed import. It is long past time for us to put these processes to use.

— Allan Creighton
Oakland, California
October 2001

preface: about this book

The original Australian edition of this book was designed with only one purpose: to provide a self-help resource for men who want to take responsibility for reducing the frequency and intensity of their anger and to eliminate the risk of reactive violence, especially in their family relationships with women and children. Since its original publication in 1999, this book has been read by thousands of men and women around Australia and New Zealand. Enthusiastic feedback from male readers and female partners confirmed that our purpose was being well served.

But something else was happening too: I began to get letters, calls, and e-mails from counselors and agencies that provide services to men who are trying to control their anger and end their violent behavior. These service providers were excited by the results they had achieved from using *Dealing with Your Anger* as a counseling text for men in group and one-on-one anger-management programs. Now they had a tool that their clients could use at home between sessions and that they could use together in sessions. Some felt that the old problem of the gap between real life and counseling sessions had finally been bridged. Others began to structure their courses for men around the book, so that each chapter provided the agenda for one or more sessions.

This edition, specially revised for publication in North America, has been carefully reworked to serve two purposes: It remains a self-help book for men. It is also a resource for practitioners, clinics, agencies, and programs that provide professional services to men trying to deal with their anger and end their violence. The content of the first edition was carefully reviewed by two professionals in the field, and at different stages of draft completion. One of those is mentioned in the acknowledgements; the other is unknown to me because his review was conducted "blind."

Since then, this book has attracted many reviews in the professional literature and the popular media. Some of these have helped to resolve the weaknesses and problems that, as with all works of this kind, inevitably laced the first edition. The contributions of two reviewers in particular have helped me improve this North American edition "out of sight," as we say in Australia:

Alan Jenkins, author of *Invitation to Responsibility: The Therapeutic Engagement of Men Who Are Violent and Abusive* (Adelaide: Dulwich, 1990) and whose critical review appeared in *Psychotherapy in Australia*, volume 6, number 3, May 2000 (Melbourne: PsycOz Publications), refocused me on the struggle for clarity over confusion.

Allan Creighton, who reviewed the original for Hunter House, the publisher that kindly offered to publish this edition, caused me to review the central messages of the book in the light of the motivation that drives violence-prevention work around the world: namely, the safety of others who might be at serious risk from our anger and violence—especially the women and children we say we care for.

I hope *Dealing with Your Anger* will be as useful to men and to professional service providers in North America as it has been to their counterparts in Australia. I hope men who read this book but find they cannot quite make the invited changes on their own will seek and be offered the professional help they need. The extensive notes at the end address the theoretical bases and practice foundations of this work.

In addition to the female counseling practitioners and related professionals, there are two broad groups of women who will want to read this book:

The first group will be female partners of men who get angry and use violence. These women will be hoping to find solutions to their partner's problems and an end to their own fear and harm. To you I say be careful: When he is angry and abusive or when you are both fighting or just "arguing," do not "offer" this book to your partner. Worse, do not just throw it at him. These are not good times for such gestures! Instead, pick a time when you are both talking calmly about his problem and how it affects you and your children. Now tell him you bought it for him and ask him to read it. By all means read it too, so you can see what he is being asked to do about his responsibility and also how this book might help. As you will see in Chapter 1, solving *his* anger problem is *his* responsibility, not yours. In fact, you can't do that for him, so don't even try.

The second group of women who might read this book are those who have a problem with their own anger. While I emphasize to you that this book was written for men, I can also tell you that many such women have found it useful for themselves. If it does no more than show you that anger is a problem that *can* be solved, and that realization prompts you either to use the exercises yourself or to seek help, then reading this book will have been worth your while. To you I say, "Go right ahead, get what you can from this book, and what you can't find here, seek elsewhere"

I hope this book is a real help to you, the reader, whoever you are—and I welcome feedback that contributes to violence prevention in a world crying out for safety and peace.

special note for counseling practitioners, health and welfare agencies, mental health clinics, veterans services, and men's violence prevention programs

This edition is a vehicle with which to transport the experiences of the counseling room or group out to the everyday world of your clients and vice versa. You can use each chapter as the set text for a one-on-one or group therapy session, or you can group some chapters into one session.

In one-on-one work, Chapters 5 and 6 must be dealt with in two consecutive sessions. In group work, experienced counselors and program staff will find they can lead people through the *Emotional BioScan for Anger* experience of Chapter 5 in a group, but then might need two or more group sessions, and even some one-on-one appointments, to help participants deal effectively with the material generated from the 'BioScan.' Cotherapists or facilitators will be especially useful here.

Chapters that quite easily group together in one session include Chapters 2 and 3, 9 and 10, and 11 and 12. Chapters 14 and 15 group well and make terrific subject material for the final group sessions in any course of *Dealing with Your Anger*.

Here are some resources that will help you first to understand the theory and practice of working with anger to prevent violence, and second to get the best from this book in your work with men:

- Donovan, F. *Power Without Control: A Social, Emotional and Practical Response to Men's Anger and Violence.* Melbourne: The Anger Clinic, 2001.

- *Dealing with Your Anger: A Reader's Workbook*

- *How to use* Dealing with Your Anger *in Clinical Practice*

- *A Practical Guide to Assessment, Planning, Counseling, and Outcome Evaluation*

- *A Twelve-Week Program for Groups in Dealing with Your Anger*
  (Includes Facilitator's Guide, Participants' Workbook and Outcome Evaluation Schedule. A series of slides for overhead or Powerpoint presentation should be available for downloading from the Internet by December, 2001)

Further information and order forms for these resources can be obtained from the author at www.angerclinic.com.au, by e-mailing him at anger_clinic@hotkey.net.au, or by mailing him at:

The Anger Clinic
PO Box 116
Mt. Macedon
Victoria 3441
Australia

acknowledgements

This book is the product of a lifetime of personal and professional struggle with anger. Since it is the product of struggle, I could not—by definition—have produced it on my own. There are so many others who made this book possible. Here are just a few:

Anne McLennan, my wife and partner, who has borne my anger over the years. Anne suffered the two years of "pregnancy" from which this book emerged and gave me all the support she could. More than that, Anne reviewed pages and pages of tedious first drafts, rewrites, and final drafts. Her contributions turned academic sociology and esoteric psychotherapy into readable text for everyday people.

My stepchildren, Elspeth and Lachlan, who put up with more than their fair share of disruption during the long "pregnancy" of this book.

Others who, in the sharing of our lives, at times have borne my anger.

The men whose stories, struggles, courage, and commitment to change are recorded in this book. To these I owe a special debt of gratitude. In many ways this book is theirs as much as mine. For the sake of their privacy and protection, I am unable to acknowledge these men publicly. Thank you, guys: I wish you well.

Rex and Vicki Finch for their faith in the original manuscript, and to Rex for his caring support and enthusiasm. Rex has a talent for encouraging me on to greater heights when I thought I'd already given my best. This book is not perfect, but it would have been well short of good enough were it not for that talent of Rex's . . . and the wisdom that fuels it.

Gerry Egan (B.A. Psych., Grad. Dip. App. Sci. [Prof. Psych.], M.A.P.S.), who provided much more than a professional review. Gerry's enthusiasm for the work, his personal and professional encouragement, his understanding of the learning process, and his vision for detail have had a huge and positive impact on the text.

I am grateful to Jeanne Brondino for her selection of the Australian edition and for her confidence in recommending that Hunter House 'take it on' in North America. I want to give recognition to the incredibly thorough copyedit that was painstakingly undertaken by Kelley Blewster. Though we might not agree on everything, so many of her contributions have improved this edition considerably. Thank you to Alex Mummery for her editorial oversight and management of the process—including some flexibility with deadlines.

Kerry Murphy, a group officer in the Country Fire Authority of Victoria and a volunteer firefighter of many years, who kindly reviewed the original draft of Part IV.

John Tame and Peter, whose time and efforts helped to make sure the book wasn't all academic and intellectual.

Wandarri, who in his own Aboriginal tradition has now been dead long enough that his name can be used, who led me to the truth that many people, when dispossessed of themselves—as were his people when dispossessed of their country—have only their anger left to drive them.

Liz Roberts, who in 1979 taught me the most important lesson I needed to be an effective change agent or difference maker: "People generally do the best they can with the internal and external resources *consciously* available to them."

Maxine Kaleb, who in 1973 taught me that *I could*, after a young life of learning that *I could not.*

And my mother, who started it all.

introduction:
a personal note

I am a man, and I get angry. The difference is I now know where it comes from and how to deal with it. These days, I don't do violent things when I get angry; I haven't for years. Even when I did, I was limited to throwing things and smashing doors, walls, and other objects. But I have hurt other people in anger, some physically (in my youth), others more emotionally and spiritually—and that's worse in some ways, because it's so disempowering. I still struggle with my anger, although my wife and family agree I have succeeded very well. But when I do get really angry (it's rare these days, thank God), I know I scare them. I don't mean to, but it happens.

So how can a man who still struggles with his own anger write a book designed to help you with your anger?

Good question!

Here's the answer.

First, I am an accredited social worker and practicing psychotherapist and counselor with over 20 years of clinical experience. If that doesn't surprise you much, this will: For the last few years, I have specialized in anger and developed a unique method of anger therapy. Clients say I am good at my job: Eighty-four percent (in the period 1996–1998) reported some level of success and major positive changes in their lives. That trend has continued to the time of writing this revision. Their parents, partners, and children reported improved relationships and a new experience of relative peace, happiness, and freedom from fear. I might be good at my job, but if you asked me to identify the critical factor that changed the lives of these men, I would point to their own courage and determination to succeed.

Second, as you have just read, I understand the struggle with anger in my own personal life. I will share that struggle with you in one or two places in this book, just as several other men will share theirs.

How have I written this book?

In two ways: as a practitioner who works with men who get angry and do violence and as a man who still struggles with his own anger and *potential* for violence.

When you get to the end, I think you will agree this is a combination that works.

dealing with
your anger…

man to man

The year before little Kelly was killed by her father in Australia, 1,500 women were killed by their husbands or boyfriends in the United States. At least 2 million American women are battered annually by an intimate partner. "Overall, the Bureau of Justice Statistics reports that women sustained about 3.8 million assaults and 500,000 rapes a year in 1992 and 1993: more than 75 percent of these violent acts were committed by someone known to the victim, and 29 percent of them were committed by an intimate—a husband, ex-husband, boyfriend or ex-boyfriend." Intimate partners accounted for about 1.25 million of these violent acts against women; a staggering level of murder and violence by men against the women they once made love with.[1]

A grateful Australia lacks the incredibly high incidence of women being murdered by their male partners that exists in the United States. But for a population of less than twenty million, our level of male violence against women is still disturbing. A survey published in 1996 found that 7.1 percent of Australian women had experienced violence in the preceding twelve months. Women were found to be more at risk from their male partners than from strangers. Of those married or living with a man, 8 percent reported an incidence of violence some time in their current relationship. Of those women who had been in a previous relationship, 42 percent reported violence by a previous partner.

And it can happen very early in a relationship (i.e., before moving in together or marrying). "An estimated 50,000 [Australian] women reported experiencing violence from a boyfriend or date during the last 12 months. Furthermore, more than one in ten women reported experiencing physical violence, and one in three sexual violence by a boyfriend or date since the age of 15 years."[2]

How much of all that in-home death and damage in America and Australia was done in anger?

Who knows?

Among police, legal, health, and social-service professionals who deal with batterers, that remains a hotly debated question.

This book is for men who get angry...so angry that they either do or threaten to do physical, verbal, or emotional violence to those around them or cause such fear that people feel they must walk on eggshells so as not to provoke their anger or the risk of violence. Although this book is useful for men who get angry and potentially violent anywhere (at work, on the road, playing sports, etc.), it is especially aimed at men who get violently or fearfully angry at home. The first objective of this book is to help men protect the women and children in their lives from the fear and risks of their violent anger. The second objective is to help men enjoy healthier and richer relationships with women, children, and other men, without their violent anger hanging like a storm cloud over the whole family.

It is also a book that will interest women, especially those who live with or have lived with angry men. While they will learn much about men's experience of their own anger, women will be encouraged to recognize and understand that **men's anger and violence are men's business—it is men who must take full responsibility for dealing with their anger and preventing their violence.** The only responsibility a man's partner has is to do what is needed to protect herself and their children from any risk his anger might pose to their physical and emotional health and safety. So let's be very clear:

No matter who's right and who's wrong, whatever the conflict between a man and a woman, whatever the behavior of a child, it is a man's responsibility alone to control his own anger and prevent his own violence. This book aims to help men do that.

Men who knowingly use their anger or violence to get what they want, to achieve some goal, or to guarantee some outcome need professional help in addition to what's in this book. For men whose first problem is what's called an attitude of entitlement—meaning they do what's needed to maintain power and control over their female partners and children (see further discussion on this issue below)—this book will not directly help them mend that attitude.

A little later we'll come back to the question of whether or not this book is right for you right now. To get to where we can better ask and answer that question we need to talk about violence itself in a little more depth. We also need to understand that, in essence, "small-scale" violence at home is no different from large-scale violence outside. Whether in warfare or wife battering, violence on any scale can be driven by anger, attitude, or both.

violence: is it anger or attitude?

The year 1994 was the International Year of the Family. It was the year Kevin East murdered his daughter, Kelly, and then killed himself. Kelly was just three years old. Murder-suicide tragedies became a frequent feature of family violence in Australia, America, and other Western countries in the dying decades of the last millennium.

Just one year after Kevin East killed little Kelly near Perth, Western Australia, Timothy McVeigh, with or without others, killed 168 people, including children, in heartland Oklahoma City. Hundreds more were injured and maimed. Eight hundred and fifty Americans were inside when the federal building was bombed—not by Arabs, Israelis, Russians, or foreign terrorists of any kind, but by fellow Americans. Gulf War veteran McVeigh was sentenced to death and executed for his part in the massacre. How many others were involved is still the subject of debate and conjecture.

What were the links between the murder of an innocent child by an Australian father who once loved her and the devastating act of war against Americans by those who loved America?

And what's it got to do with you as a man, your anger, and the women and children in your life?

Well, extreme though their violent actions were, Kevin East and the Oklahoma bombers seemed to share three things in common with a lot of other men I've known and worked with—including myself until recent years. First, they all shared what is sometimes called an *attitude of entitlement*, whereby they saw themselves—as men—having not just a right but a compulsion to control, direct, and "speak for" the lives of others around them. They even assumed a right to injure, maim, or kill in vengeance. Second, when their attitude of entitlement was challenged, constrained, or defied somehow, they became bitterly *angry* and resentful. Although outwardly calm and in control—at least during the planning and execution of their violence—they seemed to have been at war within themselves. Third, they *blamed others* for "pushing" them to violence, rather than themselves as free agents responsible for their own devastating choices. In other words, they accepted no personal responsibility.

When East killed baby Kelly, he blamed his estranged wife for leaving him, restricting his access to Kelly, and "forcing" him to punish her for her transgressions. When McVeigh was to be sentenced for the bombing in Oklahoma City, his defense stated that since the bombing was a retaliation for the previous sieges at Waco and Ruby Ridge and since Americans did not prevent those terrible and bloody tragedies, then all Americans bore some responsibility for McVeigh's bombing of the federal building in Oklahoma City.[3]

An attitude of entitlement, feelings of intense anger (not always outwardly visible), and an automatic tendency to blame someone else are common to many perpetrators of violent crime.

Former New Zealand police officer and criminologist Bill O'Brien analyzed nine mass murders and sketched another five committed around the world between 1966 and 1999.[4] He traced the terrible deaths of over 200 men, women, and children and as many again injured at the hands of mass murderers. His study ends with the massacre of students and a teacher by two fellow students at Columbine High School in Littleton, Colorado, on 20 April 1999. Most, but not all, of the assassins either killed themselves afterwards or were killed by police acting to end the carnage. Here are the lessons we men can gain from his study:

- All the killers were men (or boys).

- All exercised an attitude of entitlement, whereby they believed that being male somehow gave them ownership of the lives of others.

- If not outwardly enraged during the planning, execution, and aftermath of their violent acts, all but one (Martin Bryant of the Port Arthur massacre in Tasmania, Australia, on 28 April 1996) seemed either to have held serious grudges (another way of saying they felt angry) leading up to their killing sprees, or to have become acutely enraged just beforehand.

- Directly or indirectly, they all blamed others for creating the circumstances that left them no alternative but violent action.

What might cause some men to feel driven to such extreme violence by these attitudes of entitlement and feelings of anger, only to blame someone else for their own lives and choices? And do these features of extreme violence have anything to do with the "ordinary" violence done by ordinary men against their female partners and children in the height of their own anger?

being a man

Part of the answer lies in our learned and taken-for-granted ideas about manhood, masculinity, and male culture. An extensive body of research now exists into the social, cultural, and gendered ways we in Western societies reproduce our ideas and beliefs about men and masculinity and women and femininity. The field is much too big to deal with here, although those so inclined might start with some of the works listed in the notes and bibliography at the end of this book.[5] The more important socialization processes that influence us are touched on a little more in Chapter 2. For now, let me ask you to read and answer the following hypothetical questions. Don't think about your answers; go with your first gut reaction, and check one box only for each question:

Your answers to these questions might tell you something about how you see yourself and how you act as a man when you relate to women, children, and other men. If you are a husband or partner, they might reveal some of the unspoken but taken-for-granted attitudes you carry with you into your relationship. You might also care to consider the effect of your attitudes on those learned from you by your sons and daughters.

Now, I'm not suggesting that all of us men are out there committing mass murder, blowing up federal buildings, or killing our children. But I am saying there are some attitudes we learn as boys and uphold as men that we live by and take into our relationships with women, children, and other men. (There are also some attitudes and values that girls learn and uphold as women that set the complementary rules for them. But that's another story—one we'll touch on in Chapter 2.) One of the most frequent complaints about men that you will

1. You live with a female partner.

☐ a. Do *you help her* with the housecleaning, laundry, ironing, and/or shopping?
☐ b. Does *she help you?*
☐ c. Does *she do it all?*
☐ d. Do *you do it all?*

2. The United States is about to be invaded, and the secretary of defense has to choose one of only two *equally qualified and experienced* military officers to command the defense of the entire country. Which officer do *you* advise him to appoint?

☐ a. 45-year-old father of two, General John Boltdown
☐ b. 45-year-old mother of two, General Anne-Marie Munro

3. The best efforts of the U.S. Air Force and Navy didn't work out, and an enemy landing along the Californian coast is imminent. Of the following three regiments of infantry based in California, which one do you send in to repel the invading force?

☐ a. a regiment of men
☐ b. a regiment of women
☐ c. a regiment of both men and women

4. You arrive home from travel a day early and discover your female partner in bed with another man. What do you do first?

☐ a. Get angry, throw him out of the house (with or without a physical beating), and then start knocking *her* around
☐ b. Get angry, tell him to leave, then tell her how much it hurts to come home and find her betraying your trust and that you need to talk about your future together, if there is one
☐ c. Fly into a rage, throw things around, and smash things
☐ d. Storm out of the room and look for a weapon

5. You coach little league. It's a practice day and there are no first-aid attendants. Nine-year-old Michael's mother is working in the snack bar, and his father is in the equipment room on the opposite side of the field. In midfield Michael takes a hit to the face; his nose is bleeding and he's crying, so you get your assistant to take him off the field. Who do you send Michael to?

☐ a. His mother
☐ b. His father

hear from women is that men seem to have a basic attitude of entitlement about the women in their lives, especially their intimate partners or wives. You may have heard your own partner or other women use different words to express the same complaint. Here are some common examples:

- "You take me for granted."

- "It feels to me sometimes that I'm just here to do your bidding."

- "All I am to you these days is a meal ticket, a bed warmer, and a door mat."

- "I don't feel like I have any control over my own life anymore, but you seem to just take control as if it's your right."

Do any of these lines—or variations on them—sound familiar? There are hundreds of ways in which women all over the world describe this attitude of entitlement held by the men in their lives. In our competitive society we actually encourage this attitude through our basic commitment to the principles of competition. When you win a deal, a game, or a job, you collect the whole prize, not just part of it. So when a woman moves in with us or when we get married, we tend to assume we've won all of her, everything she's got, everything she does or can do. It goes like this:

developing an attitude of entitlement toward women

When a heterosexual man sees a woman, the first thing he finds himself doing is assessing her sexual attractiveness and potential. If his assessment is favorable, he'll then do some fantasizing about what it might be like to have sex with her. Wherever the actual relationship goes from there— i.e., working colleague, lawyer/client, doctor/patient, employer/

employee, sexual partner, or (eventually) husband/wife—initially, at least, it is her physical sexuality that confronts him and to which, one way or another, he responds. Hence the popular accusation that men treat women as sex objects.

Indeed, on seeing a woman for the first time, the burning question about her for many men is not "Who is she and what does she think, feel, and do?" but "Do I want what's she got and can I have it?" That question speaks to the whole game of chasing, competing, and winning: chasing the woman, competing with other men for her sexual, romantic, and caregiving favors . . . and winning them. For men it's a game of conquest: "I won this woman; I have a right to her and to all she has!" So develops an attitude of entitlement.

keeping the secret

If an intimate relationship does actually develop, many men extend their attitude of entitlement to include the woman's potential to meet their other, more secret needs—to be cared for physically, domestically, and emotionally. Of course, there's a powerful and painful contradiction there; our sexual attraction to a woman, and hers to us, is magic indeed. But that "need to be cared for" directly challenges our self-image of rugged strength and manly independence. It's a little bit like this: "I do need her to care for me . . . but *without her or anyone else actually knowing I do.*" To many men, this subterfuge is important in maintaining control in our relationships. Indeed, we may well lose that control if she ever gets to know that our need arises because we're not nearly so strong or independent as we once wanted her to believe. To protect this subterfuge, we maintain a façade of strength, rightness, and a superior level of knowing that in turn works to reinforce our attitude of entitlement.

And there's a bigger problem: Over time, we might be able to let our guards down a bit with her. I mean, since she is a woman she'll understand all that emotional stuff, won't she?

But what if she blabs? We could never afford to risk our friends or other men getting to know how much we need to be cared for. They'd think we were weak, under her thumb, a real pussycat! That would finish us; as men, we'd never again be able to hold our heads up in the world of men.

So where does it all come from, this attitude of entitlement? Well, it didn't just come up out of nowhere; attitudes are not biologically transmitted, and you won't find a male entitlement gene in your chromosomes. Attitudes are *socially* transmitted and learned; that means we pick up our basic attitudes about life while growing up among our parents, family, relatives, friends, the circles in which we move, and the society in which we live. To an extent, our attitudes are fostered by the media, advertising, entertainment, education, religion, politics, sports, and so on. Mostly, those attitudes get either reinforced or challenged in our interactions with other people throughout life—with men, women, colleagues, teammates, buddies, etc.

aggressive competition breeds attitude, anger, and violence

In our Western societies, starting in grade school (in Australia we call it primary school), the first, basic, and essential rule we all learn is that we must compete—for attention, for grades, for goals and points, etc. Sure, we learn to cooperate with each other; being a team player is a big deal these days. But cooperation is not the essence of the game; it just is not on the same level of importance as competition. The bottom line in all pursuits—in politics, business, education, work, sports, and sex—is to win at all costs.

Sadly, the first thing most men want to do with other men is to judge them for their ability to compete effectively for physical, sexual, and occupational superiority. Men can be skilled at many activities and valued for all sorts of qualities at home, at work, in cinema, theatre, art, or music, etc. But first and foremost, even if not always able to win first prize, "real men" are recognized by their ability to put up a good fight, to compete aggressively, to stay in the game. On the sexual front, "real men" are supposed to win the most attractive women—the ones most sought after, for whom other men pant. Having competed and won, we feel entitled to the spoils of victory—all of them! So the problem we have is that our economy, society, and culture are all based upon aggressive competition, and that creates the preconditions for violence.

Since most of that violence is done by men, it is up to us to stop it—or at least to stop it from getting worse. To do that, we need to understand how violence, or at least the potential for violence, is woven into our society and culture, through our preoccupation with competition and the attitude of entitlement that grows from it. Let's take a look at two very public areas of activity in which we can see attitudes of entitlement and the potential for violence at work in everyday life.

First, take politics. Have you ever listened to the cut and thrust of debate in a legislature, on TV or radio, or during election campaigns? I spent six years of my life in the public spotlight of politics—as a legislator in an Australian state parliament. Believe me, the language there was all about belittling and ridiculing your opponents, blaming the other side for everything, trying always to expose them in some criminal act or corrupt practice. The unwritten rule was "never apologize; never admit you're wrong." The primary objective was to inflict as much public damage, injury, or harm as you could upon the other side. For example, ask the political backroom boys this question: "Was it more important whether former president Bill Clinton actually had sex with 'that woman,' or whether his opponents could create a compelling _perception_ that he had done so?" Now, maybe Clinton was guilty as hell; I don't know. But I do know that for his enemies the perception was much more important than the performance. The creation of negative perceptions about people in public life can destroy them in the public's eye. And that is violence! Yet, in all democratic countries of the West, it is a practice to which politicians and others are not just entitled, but that they are actively encouraged to pursue.

It is violence because it is behavior that sets out maliciously to do damage, harm, or injury to the person instead of showing the person's actions, opinions, or point of view on an issue to be wrong or insufficient. In other words, it becomes a case of shoot the messenger instead of the message. And that might be because the doers of this kind of violence—frequently our political leaders—do not like the messenger or the message or because the message hurts or shows the unpleasant truth of a situation. So, violence is used here as an attempt to use power and control abusively and unfairly so that only one side of a story gets heard. There is a special responsibility that falls on those elected to legislate against violence: "Do not yourselves *use* violence as a primary tool of political debate in your legislatures or on the television sets of the nation. For when you do so, you send a message that violence really is ok after all!"

The same responsibility falls upon parents at home: Degrading name-calling, emotional abuse and manipulation, unfairly restricting someone's freedom of movement and association with others, 'stalking,' belittling, and so on are all forms of violence. When you use these kinds of violence against your partner or children, you say to the children, "It's ok." A goal of this book is not just to help the reader stop doing physical harm to persons or property, but also to help him stop doing emotional and spiritual harm to a person's very selfhood.

Now let's take a look at sports like Football, Australian Rules Football, Rugby Union, and so on, where aggression and violence are major features of the game. Even where these features are officially outlawed, this particular form of violence—this "over the top" aggression—is encouraged in the language and imagery of promotional advertising and live commentary, and by spectators themselves.

The new rule for male athletes and sportsmen is "Give 'em hell and give it often!" Or, as overheard on one football training ground, "Are you a bunch of girls? Let's get some attitude round here—this is war!" Then there was that widely reported attitude of an American swimming star towards his Australian rivals just before the 2000 Sydney Olympics: "We're gonna smash 'em like guitars." And what about that young Australian tennis ace with his "trademark" aggressive finger punch to the face televised so often to the world? What you can't hear are the expletives that go with it.

Can you see the attitudes and the potential for violence in politics and sports? Remember this: Politics and sports don't just help to shape the way we live; they also accurately mirror the dominant attitudes and behavior at work in our everyday lives.

shame, anger, and violence

There's a big price to be paid by both men and women for our rigid conformity to market rules, and to ingrained ideas about manhood and about men and women. What happens when men and women don't quite measure up, when they fail to win, when she can't keep her husband or protect the children, when he can't keep a job or "control" his wife? If they're lucky they get to a counselor or therapist and start the long or short, but always painful, process of rebuilding their self-esteem and confidence, or of learning how to live without controlling and winning all the time. Most can't afford therapy or don't get referred; so they muddle on. Women often experience a kind of guilt-induced depression that's hard to break out of. Some men experience a cycle of guilt and anger that leads to depression or despair and even suicide.

More often, men experience a cycle of shame and anger that leads them to violent behavior. Their violence might be acted out upon objects (walls, doors, furniture, ornamental objects, cars), against themselves (drinking, driving fast, self-injury, self-mutilation), or against other people—usually intimate relations (partners, children, relatives, parents)—with the high risk of serious harm and the possibility of death.

Yet, we never really get to recognize, own, or deal with our shame, do we? More often than not, men's counterreaction to shame is so fast that they don't actually have time to experience this painful emotion at all. That's because many men learn early in life a distorted version of that "sacred" code of manhood: *death before dishonor.* We learn that the very worst thing to risk is not death but shame—a distortion of what is meant by *dishonor.* As men, we learn that it is deeply shameful to be exposed and humiliated as weak, cowardly, dependent, not in control of life, in need of care, a loser, etc. Therefore, shame is not experienced for more than an instant, not allowed into a "real" man's experience for longer than it takes *anger* to rise up and fight it, to protect our fragile manhood.

To understand how shame can work so powerfully in men, let's turn to an expert for a moment. Dr. James Gilligan worked with the worst of violent men held in forensic psychiatric hospitals and state penitentiaries in Massachusetts. Included in Dr. Gilligan's twenty-five years of working with America's most violent criminals was his time as medical director of the Bridgewater State Hospital for the criminally insane and as director of mental health for the Massachusetts prison system.[6]

A recitation of Gilligan's qualifications includes the following: "The Massachusetts prison system brought him in because of the high suicide and murder rates within the prisons. When he left ten years later, the rates of both had dropped to virtually zero."[7] I guess that means he knows something about violence that we all could learn from. Here's what Gilligan says about men in America: "We have a horror of dependency in this country—particularly dependency on the part of men. No wonder we have so much violence—especially male violence. For the horror of dependency is what causes violence. The emotion that causes the horror of dependency is shame."[8]

In his extensive work with America's most violent men, Gilligan discovered that shame causes hate—an expression of burning anger—and that guilt turns shame inward on a person's self. Shame, then, tends to generate violence against other people, whereas guilt tends to generate violence against the self. So what makes violence such an overwhelmingly male thing to do?

Some have argued that it has to do with male chemistry—specifically our testosterone. Others have argued that it is instinctual—part of our evolutionary and genetic inheritance. From the most violent of men in America's prisons, Gilligan learned the truth about the so-called "instinct theory" of male violence:

> It enables some men (especially violent men) to hide their most shameful secret, namely, that violence is not an innate, authentic part of men's inborn human nature, but serves instead as a smoke screen that hides the unacceptable, "unmanly" desire to be taken care of—wishes, which if gratified, would make many a man feel that he was passive, dependent, infantile and weak, that is to say, "not a man."[9]

The need to dominate and the need to be taken care of seem to contradict each other, don't they? Perhaps that explains the violent tension some of us feel in our guts much of the time.

Very close to that "secret" need to be taken care of, and substituting for it in a way that men can be comfortable with, is our need to be recognized, respected, and included (in the group). Indeed, to be *excluded*, especially in ways that bring upon us great public shame, is to invite a lasting, deep, and burning anger.

Let's look at what happened at Columbine High School in Littleton, Colorado, on 20 April 1999. According to O'Brien, one of the factors that so shamed and then enraged the two young killers, Klebold and Harris, was their exclusion from the mainstream of strong, competitive young sportsmen—the "jocks"—and their ridicule by fellow male and female students who were part of the "in crowd." The other was their consequent determination to be different in behavior and dress, so they could stand out and be counted as "men" in their own right, rather than as weak victims of a system that made pariahs of them.[10] Their identification as "trenchcoat mafia" helped emphasize their difference; it also served to incubate still further their anger and hostility to the point of mass murdering their youthful antagonists.

bombing or battering— what's the difference?

By now you're no doubt asking, "What's the link Donovan's trying to make between *me* and a man who killed his child, the Oklahoma bombers, and all those mass murderers?" And you might be saying, "Look, buddy, all I do is get angry and throw a couple of things around, and maybe I hit her or push her around once or twice—in a rage." Well I want you to take this in and think about it:

Violence on the scale of that committed by East, McVeigh, or young Klebold and Harris is but the extreme outer rim of an ordinary cycle of violence. We feel the need to be taken care of and to belong, but our codes of manhood shame us deeply if we're not in control and independent. Our attitudes help protect us from shame. But when our attitudes are challenged by reality, we get angry—and sometimes violent.

Thank God there are three differences between mass murder and *most* episodes of male family violence: the scale, the intent, and the outcome. Of course, we can't afford to forget that every year, approximately 1,500 American women are killed by their husbands or boyfriends. As men, it falls to us to break this cycle of violence and guarantee safety for the women and children in our lives.

so is it attitude or anger?

You've probably figured out the answer by now. Violence can be used to get our own way and to enforce our will—a strategic expression of an *attitude of entitlement*. Or, violence can be generated in the height of rage—a reaction to *anger*. And, of course, it can be driven by both attitude and anger at once.

What should you do then—deal with your attitudes or your anger?

Since our aim here is to help men prevent violence by dealing with their anger, that's another way of asking whether or not this book is the right one for you right now. We'll try to answer that question.

is this book for you right now?

You might have one or more of the following reasons for reading this book:

- Violent or not, you have a problem with your anger.

- You live with or know a man who gets violently angry.

- You work professionally with men who get angry and violent.

- You train or educate health or social service professionals.

- You manage a health or social service agency, clinic, or program.

- You have an interest in the area of anger and violence prevention.

Whatever made you open this book, it is important that you read this section, because there are important issues raised here that every reader should understand—even if he or she disagrees with me about them.

Many men have already used *Dealing with Your Anger* on their own to make great and lasting changes in their lives and relationships. Many others have taken the book to a professional counselor, agency, or clinic to get help with the change work that needs to be done. Many counselors are using this book as an aid to their work, even prescribing it to their clients as essential reading. Other professionals are using it as the basis for group programs for men, setting "homework" assignments for participants and using the chapters as agenda material for group meetings. But the book has limitations, some of which will be obvious; two are critical enough to be spelled out here.

The first critical limitation is straightforward. Some men pose a serious risk to their partners and children; your first responsibility is to eliminate that risk. We'll talk more about risk assessment and reduction in the next section of this chapter. But right now, it is really important that if you think your risk is too high, or if you're not sure you can fix your anger problem with a book alone, *get help!* That's right, get on the telephone right now and find a resource for men's information or a hotline that can put you in touch with an agency, clinic, or men's program in your area. Make an appointment, take this book along with you, and say you want help to work through it. Or, ask what other programs are offered that you could enroll in.

The second critical limitation is a little more complicated and, if not confronted and sorted out, leaves unresolved a major threat to the safety of women and children. So, I need to put this just right. There are some men who *know* they won't stop their violence just by reading a book on anger, men who *choose* to use violence. *They, too, need to get professional help; this book alone will not guide them to making the necessary changes.*

Let me put it simply: As I've already suggested, some men use violence to gain or keep power and control over their wives or partners, to get their own way or to achieve some outcome. I call that *strategic violence*—and it can include the use of anger itself as a violent strategy. Let's be straight about this: Anyone who has been angry knows that we can also make ourselves angry or sound and behave as though we were angry—if it suits our ends. Men who knowingly use violence strategically, and that includes using anger as a means of control (we'll talk more about that in Chapter 3), will need more than this book to help them meet their responsibilities for the safety of women and children in their lives. That's because they are being driven more by their attitude of entitlement (as we discussed it in the previous section) than they are by their emotion of anger. Do you see the difference?

Let's go back to Kelly's dad, Kevin East, and see if his story can help.

After the tragedy of the murder–suicide, *The West Australian* newspaper reported receiving a letter to the editor written by East before he killed Kelly and himself. In the letter, he had complained of insufficient access to Kelly awarded by the Family Court of Australia, and he said he "wanted to punish his former de facto wife for the pain he had suffered."[11] In an audiocassette tape he sent to the same paper, East said, "these are the consequences of hurting me, and she [Kelly's mother] has to suffer" and "she has to be punished and I believe I have the right to punish her."[12]

The tape revealed many disturbing features of East's former relationship:

- East accepted no blame or responsibility for his part in the breakdown of his relationship with his former partner.

- He claimed himself to be the "victim" of their relationship.

- He obsessed about dates and times of events that occurred in the relationship.

– He accused his former partner of a number of "transgressions" that he believed he had the right to discipline and change as he saw fit.

– He blamed her for his "bad" feelings and career failures.

– He accused her of "worming her way into his life and his house."

– He blamed her for everything, saying that if she had just done what he wanted, things would have been okay.

According to subsequent investigations by experts, East had expected full conformity with his wishes, opinions, and decisions. What part this attitude of entitlement played in the couple's separation can only be guessed. Certainly it was strong enough that East was unable to accept the "shame" of being opposed, of maybe even being wrong, of losing control not only of his partner and their relationship but also of access to their daughter. An academic and expert on family violence, Jenny Gardiner, had this to say in concluding her analysis of Kevin East's murder-suicide tape: "This tape was not made by someone in a moment of grief or passion. It was made by someone who was rational, (but) who was obsessed."[13]

Can you see the difference here? Kevin East held an iron-strong attitude of entitlement that was challenged in the end by his former partner and rejected by the family court. East then chose to murder his daughter to stop them from winning and to punish his wife. Whether it was fear of retribution, his accurate forecast of the shame he would endure, or both that led him to suicide, we can only guess.

So ask yourself now, "How is it in my relationship?" If you use violence or commit violence, which of the following two scenarios best describes how it happens in your relationship?

Scenario 1: You get angry and start to throw things around the house. You smash things or start swinging your fists, punching walls and doors in your growing rage. Or you start striking out against your partner or children—a slap here, a punch there, or just throwing them down on the floor or against furniture or a wall. You get into such an uncontrollable rage that you don't know what you're doing or what harm you've done until later. Finally, you exhaust yourself and calm down; now you can at last see the harm and damage you've done. That's when the shame sets in and you flare up all over again. Or the shame starts to turn into feelings of guilt, and you become suicidal, get in the car and drive like a maniac, or drink yourself into oblivion.

Is that the way it is? Or is it more like the following?

Scenario 2: You're in control of what *you* are doing, but you need to reassert your control over your partner, or the kids, or the family as a whole. You use simple coercion, strength of argument, emotional or rational domination to "get things straight around here." Or you appeal to your "authority as the man": You just present an air of rightness, of just knowing what's right because of your expertise or knowledge about whatever is at issue. So you use your strengths and power as a man to assert your control at home. When they still don't comply, and knowing the fear your anger causes in your partner and children, that's when you "stage a rage" for them. Or when it all fails, and you need some "real enforcement," you turn to physical force or violence to get what you want. Or maybe you just skip all the stages and go straight to physical force to have your way in the first place. Is this more like how it is?

- If your anger is like scenario 1, but you don't reach the violent stage of harm or fear to your partner and children or damage to your home, this book will help you deal with it. You will do better with a skilled counselor or in a group, but many men have succeeded by working through the book on their own.

- If your anger is like scenario 1, including doing harm to or creating fear in those around you or doing damage to your home, you are strongly advised to get professional help while you work through this book. Ideally, this would be with a professionally trained and skilled psychotherapist or counselor (e.g., a social worker, psychologist, or someone with similar qualifications), but it could be with a minister of religion who has qualifications in psychotherapy or counseling. Or you could get help from a health or social service agency or clinic, or a men's program.

- If your problem is more like scenario 2, then you need more than this book can offer you by itself. You have a serious attitude of entitlement by which you expect and enforce compliance with your will. You need outside help. Your partner and children have a right to expect you to go and get that help. Your partner has an obligation to your children and herself to leave you if you do not take responsibility for stopping your violence. What gets me and others who work in this field is this: Your partner may well stay because she is too scared of what you will do if she leaves. And don't fool yourself; it's not just for herself she's scared—it's for your children! Look what happened to little Kelly East. If it weren't for her dad and his attitude of entitlement, she would be past age ten when you read this.

Now, it is true that in the course of working with men's anger, I have found that these types of men go on to challenge their old attitudes and beliefs about men, women, and relationships. But that's been while working either one-on-one with a professional or in groups of men, where attitudes can be challenged while change is being supported. A book is different. If you're only reading a book, you can kid yourself if you want to; no one is ever going to know. But you will likely still go on knocking around your wife or partner, and the kids will still get scared of you. The only thing your whole family will agree on is that this book failed them, that nothing changed, and that their lives are still hell.

And they'd be right.

If you've got an *attitude* problem that you're trying to kid yourself is an *anger* problem, get on the phone to a men's hotline; ask for a batterers' program or a men's violence-prevention group. You can always put this book on the shelf until you've dealt with your attitude and you're ready to deal with your anger.

If, on the other hand, you really do have an *anger* problem, let's get some idea of how bad it is and how much of a risk you are to your family and the people around you. The risk assessment that follows should help you do that.

assessing your risk of doing harm or damage

First, I have to say that there is no well-developed, surefire formula for assessing accurately the risk of men doing harm to their wives, female partners, or children. It is not like the weather. You can't forecast violence the way you can forecast hurricanes, although the outcome can be tragically similar—as the people of Oklahoma City and Littleton, Colorado, know only too well.

Second, I have to recommend that the best way to get an assessment of your volatility and risk to your partner and children is to seek the advice of a professional counselor or agency that provides services for men who are trying to deal with their anger and violence. I understand that not all readers will be able or willing to do that right now.

For men who want to assess for themselves their level of risk to their partners and children, I have presented below a self-assessment tool called the Anger Volatility Index, or AVI. Again, the AVI is not a certain way of judging your risk; it is indicative only. It's a little like the Richter scale for earthquakes—you can read how bad it was afterwards, but not how bad it will be beforehand. What you *can* do is whatever it takes to guarantee protection for those likely to be harmed by your violent anger.

The AVI comes from the anger-control signals (see Chapter 3) reported by twenty-five men selected at random from those who worked with me to reduce and control their anger. Basically, the more volatile your anger, the more risk you pose to those around you—especially your wife, partner, or girlfriend and children.

To complete your AVI, follow these steps:

Work your way through the AVI, starting at the lowest level of anger, level 1, and working through to the highest level of anger recorded here, level 4. As you go, check the box beside each phrase that you feel applies to you *when you get angry.* Don't think about it; just go with your gut—if you find yourself saying "Yeah, that's me," check the box. If you find yourself saying "That's close, but not quite me," still check the box. If the phrase does not fit for you in any way at all when you are angry, leave it blank.

At the end of each level, you'll find a question: "Is this as bad as it gets?" You must answer yes or no. First, look through the phrases in the next level to see if any apply to you.

If you answer "no" to the question "'Is this as bad as it gets?" you must keep going, carefully checking all the phrases that apply to you in the higher levels. Leave blank those you don't recognize at all.

If you do not recognize any phrases in any of the higher levels, answer "yes," and go straight to the chart labeled "Your Anger Volatility Index," on page 36. There you can record your AVI rating by checking the box beside the level where you stopped. Then take the minimum and recommended actions indicated for your AVI level. You have to feel *100 percent confident* that none of the remaining phrases apply to you before you quit working through the levels.

The level you check on the AVI chart is your level of volatility. The higher your AVI level, the greater the risk you pose to your wife, partner or girlfriend, and children.

anger volatility index

Start at level 1, and work down until you answer "yes" *with 100 percent confidence* to the question "Is this as bad as it gets?" Then quit and turn to the chart labeled "Your Anger Volatility Index," on page 36.

anger volatility index: level 1

☐ I start to shuffle my feet.

☐ I feel emotionally tense.

☐ I fidget.

☐ I feel churned up.

☐ My body feels tense.

☐ My breathing gets shallow.

☐ I bottle up my emotions and stress.

☐ I start feeling frustrated.

☐ I feel irritated.

☐ I get knots in my gut.

☐ My speech gets clipped and tight.

☐ I make cutting comments.

☐ I want to control the situation.

☐ My legs get tensed up.

☐ I feel pressure in my head.

☐ I feel pressured by her or the kids.

☐ I become distant, moody, and start brooding.

Is this as bad as it gets?

☐ **YES**

☐ **NO**   **Proceed to Level 2 Signals**

anger volatility index: level 2

☐ I breathe more quickly.

☐ I make demands and commands.

☐ I move about quickly.

☐ I feel tension across my chest, back, and shoulders.

☐ I glare viciously.

☐ I get agitated.

☐ My pulse rate goes up.

☐ I have to move.

☐ My voice gets louder.

☐ My speech gets faster.

☐ I feel more churned up.

☐ I feel sorry for myself.

☐ I clench my fists.

☐ I clench my teeth.

☐ I start locking my jaw.

☐ My frustration goes up.

☐ I start to feel strong.

☐ I start pointing my finger.

☐ I start making sharp hand gestures.

☐ My voice tone and volume rise.

☐ I wave my arms around.

☐ I start making jolting movements.

☐ My blood pressure goes up.

☐ The blood vessels in my neck swell.

☐ I feel unstable.

- ☐ My palms and feet sweat.
- ☐ The back of my neck gets tight.
- ☐ I have emotional flashbacks.
- ☐ My head aches.
- ☐ My temples throb.
- ☐ I stand over people.
- ☐ I say things to hurt.
- ☐ I feel nasty.
- ☐ My muscles feel tight.
- ☐ I feel like a caged animal.
- ☐ I feel self-pity.
- ☐ I feel contempt.
- ☐ I bang things.
- ☐ I grab things tightly.

Is this as bad as it gets?

- ☐ **YES**
- ☐ **NO**   **Proceed to Level 3 Signals**

anger volatility index: level 3

- ☐ Things start to happen fast.
- ☐ I feel numb in my head.
- ☐ I start stomping around.
- ☐ My skin feels tight.
- ☐ I shout.
- ☐ I feel hate.
- ☐ I lash out.

- ☐ I yell.
- ☐ I boil over with rage.
- ☐ My stomach turns.
- ☐ I breathe heavily.
- ☐ My heart races.
- ☐ I curse and swear.
- ☐ I want to hit and kick.
- ☐ My voice gets loud and strong.
- ☐ I feel really strong now.
- ☐ My adrenaline pumps.
- ☐ I grind my teeth.
- ☐ I feel like I start to lose control.
- ☐ I feel like smashing things up.
- ☐ I want to unleash.
- ☐ My heart beats strongly.
- ☐ I feel breathless.
- ☐ My face and head feel hot.
- ☐ I refuse to stop.
- ☐ My speech gets louder and/or more clipped.
- ☐ My stomach feels hollow.
- ☐ I throw things.
- ☐ I feel the energy.
- ☐ I feel like I must fight.
- ☐ I feel hated by the world.
- ☐ My eyes blaze.

- [ ] I feel agitated in my face.

- [ ] I sweat.

- [ ] I blame the other person.

- [ ] I grab, push, or attack in some way.

- [ ] I bang and slam things.

- [ ] I break out of my cage.

- [ ] I get sick satisfaction at frightening the other person.

- [ ] I feel like a taut spring.

- [ ] I want to hit someone.

- [ ] I want to destroy.

- [ ] I feel a need for physical release.

Is this as bad as it gets?

- [ ] **YES**

- [ ] **NO**   **Proceed to Level 4 Signals**

anger volatility index: level 4

- [ ] My anger erupts like a volcano.

- [ ] I lose focus.

- [ ] I get that "too late" feeling.

- [ ] I hit something.

- [ ] I hit somebody.

- [ ] I punch walls.

- [ ] I punch someone.

- [ ] I snarl.

- [ ] I become aggressive physically.

- [ ] I feel enraged.

☐ My voice gets wilder and I yell abuse and threats.

☐ I feel like I reach explosion point.

☐ I cut myself off from reason.

☐ I feel calm and cold.

☐ I feel hateful and vindictive.

☐ I abuse her.

☐ I feel my arms get charged with energy.

☐ I walk towards my target.

☐ I go silent.

☐ My voice erupts volcanically.

☐ My body feels exhausted.

☐ My temples feel like they will explode.

☐ I slam my hands down.

☐ I lose control of my emotions.

☐ I want to smash wedding photos and other things.

☐ I see myself but I can't stop.

☐ I feel lost or blacked out.

☐ I smash things.

☐ I throw things.

☐ I throw her.

☐ I kick things.

☐ I kick her.

☐ I threaten her or the kids.

☐ I intimidate her or the kids.

☐ I don't care anymore.

☐ I feel like I am losing control.

☐ I rage verbally.

☐ I feel a heat rush to the top of my head.

☐ War rages inside me as I try to stop.

☐ I feel desperate.

☐ I stop feeling pain.

☐ I behave like a volcano.

Is this as bad as it gets?

☐ **YES**

☐ **NO**   **It gets worse than this.**

If your Anger Volatility Index (AVI) rating is level 3 or higher, you should follow the directions at the very beginning of this book, under the heading "What You Should Do Now." If you have already moved out of home while you work to solve your anger and violence problem, congratulations! You have taken the first step in your responsibility for the safety of the women and children in your life, and you are ready to start work on solving your problem. I repeat, at your level of risk, it is highly recommended that you get professional help in working your way through the next chapters in this book. If you have not taken that step, you are urged to do so now—what happens to your wife, partner or girlfriend, and children at your hands when you are angry is your responsibility. Do what you must to guarantee their safety *today*!

If your AVI is lower than level 3, you should finish reading this chapter, take a break (no more than one day), and start Chapter 2. You can follow the process and complete the tasks, chapter by chapter, from there. Again, if you have any doubt about your ability to make the changes you need from working with this book alone, you, too, should seek professional help. And, whether you do or don't have such doubts, skilled professional help while you work through this book is recommended anyway.

In the next and final section of this chapter, we'll take a snapshot of what's in the rest of the book: what to expect, what not to expect, and the order of work.

the challenge

Dealing with Your Anger is the outcome of some twenty-five years of personal and professional struggle with the problem of anger. You will not find here an intellectual or political recipe for changing the world, however cruel it is, however much it makes you angry. There is much about the world that I get angry at; there is much I find hostile and alienating. The emotional and spiritual alienation of modern humans has its roots in two hundred years of economic, political, and social revolution—including the massive technological revolution of our own age. Neither you nor I can change that on our own. But if men (and women) collectively took on our emotional alienation with as much enthusiasm as we embrace intellectual challenges, profound changes would occur in the ways we relate to ourselves, those close to us, and the world around us. Imagine the powerful force for positive change that could be unleashed if men and women could integrate their intellectual selves with their emotional selves, instead of attempting to crush the one with the other.

Neither will you find here a sophisticated behavioral or cognitive psychology. True, the field of psychology offers much upon which this book draws. But it draws even more heavily upon the changes experienced by many clients in therapy over the years.

Most importantly, this is the work of one man—who struggled with his own anger—offered to other men as they search for encouraging ways to change their lives. You see, my work as a therapist has been the source of my professional

your anger volatility index

anger levels		action indicated	
Anger levels	Check the highest level that applies	Minimum action you must take	Additional action recommended
Level 1	☐	Finish this chapter, then turn to Chapter 2.	Outside support will help, e.g., a counselor.
Level 2	☐	Finish this chapter, then turn to Chapter 2.	Getting help with the book from a skilled professional or agency is highly recommended.
Level 3	☐	Get help working through this book from a skilled professional or agency.	Consider moving out until you can guarantee safety. See "What You Should Do Now," on page vii.
Level 4	☐	1. Follow the directions in "What You Should Do Now," on page vii, and move out until you are guaranteed safe. 2. Get help with this book from a skilled professional or agency.	As well as following this book, you may get more benefit by joining a men's group program that helps men deal with anger and stop using violence.
Higher than 4	☐	Move out now. Then follow level 4 minimum and recomended actions.	

development, specialization, and success with my clients. In that sense, this book is more a product of their work than it is of mine. Originally, though, it was my own struggle with my own anger that motivated me to write. You will be exposed to that struggle, as you will be to the struggles of many other ordinary men, throughout this book. Please use that exposure to help yourself through the challenging work ahead.

You will find this a very human book, and, I hope, a very helpful one. It is human because it speaks to actual human experience from the point of view of the angry. It is helpful because angry men can actually use this book to attempt the sorts of positive changes my clients have made in therapy.

Chapters 2 and 3 help angry men (and the women around them) to answer some basic but largely unspoken questions about anger. Just what is anger really (when you strip it of all the political, legal, psychological, psychiatric, and even religious debates that surround this most human emotion)? What are the vital differences between *anger* and *violence*? What are some of the things other men get angry at?

The rest of the book is devoted to emotional healing and practical change. Specifically, it sets out to provide you with some answers to the question "What can I do to stop myself from getting so angry?"

Chapters 4, 5, and 6 develop some personal and creative ways for you to heal your anger, experience better emotional health, and find a level of internal peace with which not only you, but the women and children around you, can live.

Chapters 7 through 13 develop some practical ways for you to control your anger—or at least to reduce the risk of doing harm to yourself, your family, and your home and possessions when you do get angry.

Chapters 14 and 15 take an altogether different and positive look at anger—it's a real energy burst. We explore some positive ways in which you can use everything you will have learned in this book. You get invited to do some creative things with your anger energy that you have probably never imagined yourself doing—the kinds of things you can do when you run your anger instead of your anger running you.

You have picked up this book because you have a problem with your anger. Can you imagine how you might turn that anger around, into an energy force for positive change? Throughout *Dealing with Your Anger* you will read about ordinary men and hear what they have done to control their anger and change their lives.[14]

Of course, a self-help book does have limits and disadvantages that face-to-face work with a therapist does not have, but please don't be put off by that. There are some advantages as well: You go at your own pace in your own time, you don't have to keep appointments that might interfere with work, and it is a lot less expensive.

The processes and strategies described in this book were developed with men in my consulting rooms. They have been formalized and modified to work for you on the printed page. Step-by-step instructions and suggestions should help you to overcome most of the obstacles you meet as you learn how to change your life.

Finally, as you will see in Chapter 5 and other places, I do not ask you to do anything I have been unwilling to do myself. As I've said, this book is the product of my own struggle with anger as much as that of my clients.

Be courageous—and welcome aboard.

chapter two

what is anger?

Man's inhumanity to man makes countless thousands mourn.[1]

— *Robert Burns*

Burns could just as truthfully have said,
"Man's inhumanity to man makes countless thousands *angry*."
And he would have been very close to the truth, for anger
is the natural emotion we humans experience in response to
a perceived threat, frustration, assault, or obstruction to our
humanity—to our sense of selfhood, or who we are. For men,
anger is our most common and immediate response to the
experience of physical or emotional pain and fear.[2]

Kevin (age 45) was angry, so was Fabian (35), and so was
Michael (25). Almost three generations of manhood were rep-
resented here, except they were unrelated and unknown to
each other. But they did have three things in common:

1. All three had been seriously angry and violent with their
   female partners: Kevin with his wife, Fabian with his
   fiancé, Michael with his girlfriend.

2. All three, by the time they got to me, were in a state of
   deep mourning. So were their partners. All three women
   had had enough and were (literally) sick with living in constant fear, intimidation, and humiliation. Somehow—and

this is so hard for most women—they each had found the strength to give their men an ultimatum: "You get fixed or I get out!"

3. All three men succeeded in dealing with their anger, using essentially the same processes you will learn.

You will meet these three men a few times in this book. You will also meet several other men who had problems with their anger.

anger versus violence

First things first. We need to make a distinction between *anger* and *violence*. Simply put, anger is an emotion; it is what we *feel*. Violence is what some of us might *do* when we are angry, or even when we are not. Violence can be physical or emotional or spiritual. But anger is what we *feel*, not what we *do*.

Because anger is an emotion, let's consider our emotions for a moment: where they come from and what we men tend to do with them.

human emotions and men

Psychologists, psychotherapists, psychiatrists, and other students of human behavior have always argued about emotions—what they are, what causes them, what purpose they serve, where they come from, and so on.[3] These days there seems to be some agreement that emotions are generated in different parts of the brain from where our thoughts are generated. What is called the limbic brain seems to be the main source of emotional response. That's the "older" part of the brain (in evolutionary terms), toward and around its base, where the brain stem departs for the neck. The neocortex (also in evolutionary terms) is the "newer" part that grows around and over the brain. You may have seen pictures of the brain, usually featuring the neocortex, where most of our rational and sensory activity occurs. Studies of evolution seem to confirm that the limbic brain developed in our prehistoric ancestors long before the neocortex and the rational faculties of modern *Homo sapiens* developed.

Our emotions, then—anger, fear, hurt, sadness, joy, and their "relatives"—seem to be evolutionary hand-me-downs that prompt us to react to events that affect or surround us in some way. Our emotional responses, in fact, are much "older" in evolutionary terms than are our intellectual or rational responses.

For us men, the practical question that comes out of all this is how do we "own" and manage our emotions in daily life? The answer for many of us is that we try to distance ourselves from our emotions, by disowning or submerging them—at least those like pain and fear, which are problematic for many of us. As kids, we learn to bottle them up; in time, we learn to bury them altogether.

burying your emotions

My mother married my father when she was in her early twenties.... When he died... [she] resolved to remain celibate for the rest of her life.

Brought up by my mother... [i.e., in an all-female home] I had many of her mannerisms and habits which... meant that I seemed effeminate to the other kids at school.

I was given a girl's name—Patricia—and ridiculed.... They could do it because I was not formidable enough to stop them, *and so the rage that I felt had to be contained.* [My emphasis.]

— *Peter McMillan in* Men, Sex and Other Secrets[4]

Those bottled up feelings come out anyway, to fuel our anger in another time and place. If we expressed *all* our deeper feelings openly, we could be less angry, less often. So what *is* all that fuelled-up anger we feel?

emotional assaults upon the self

The anger we feel is our natural emotional response to our experience (or perception) of threat, assault or attack, harm, frustration, or obstruction. These experiences can be physical, emotional, intellectual, or spiritual. I call such experiences "assaults upon our selfhood" or "assaults upon the self"[5] because they challenge and diminish our sense of who we are, what we can do, and who we can become. Cutting off large parts of our emotional selves and potentials is one of the most destructive "assaults" we can suffer.[6] Yet we men do it to ourselves daily, the way others did it to us as we grew up.

what is a "self"?

Before we talk further about assaults upon the self, we need to get clear about this whole concept of "self" and just what it is.

My "self" is who *I* am in relation to all the other people in the world around me. It has often been described as "the 'I' of me."[7] I'm sure it's just coincidence that, in English, *I* is also the first letter of the words *inside* and *internal*; my "self" refers to who I am inside, not necessarily who you see on the outside.

Outwardly, I see and hear you through my eyes and ears. But inside I see you through the "video camera" of my experience of you—and of all the other people, events, and experiences of my life so far. I have an emotional biography, a book of "I" to which I keep adding new lines, paragraphs, and chapters. But it is more than a biography, this story of who I have been and what I have done. In this internal book of "I" are also my expectations, hopes, and fears of what is still to come in my life, and who I am yet to become.

Carl Rogers, acknowledged as the father of American psychotherapy, put it this way: "It appears that the goal the individual most wishes to achieve, the end which he knowingly and unknowingly pursues, is to become himself."[8]

building your "self"

The message is that I keep on becoming who I am until I die. Life is a project that we need to take charge of, if it is to be our own project. But it isn't as simple as that, because we did not start our own life project—our parents did that. Nor did we get to write, on our own and unaided, the early and most formative chapters of our life project. All sorts of people—mostly but not exclusively adults—had a hand in that. So, when it came to our own life and our "selfhood" in it, we did not start with our own blank slate. Rather, we "took over" our life project, progressively, bit by bit, as we grew up. And even as adults, it seems sometimes hard to accept that we now have total control. I guess that is because in lots of ways we are still engaged with others whose approval, acceptance, respect, and love we crave.

What we come to believe, think, feel, and do as adults is often mapped out for us as children. The sorts of values and beliefs we are taught and encouraged to accept are learned from parents, teachers, other adults, and other kids. (You know about peer pressure!) This learning does not happen just in classrooms, but in church, on playing fields, in locker rooms and swimming pools, in gangs and groups, and so on. In fact, our learning continues through all our experiences—good and bad—in interaction with other people and events.

Music, sports, entertainment, the media, advertising, formal education, religious practice—all of our interactive experiences with the world around us—have big impacts upon the image of ourselves that we try to present: our social image.[9] The process of learning to present an acceptable social image of who we are supposed to be is called socialization. And girls and women experience socialization in a different way from how boys and men experience it.

male self, female self

Even today, the sort of social image many in our society expect a woman to present includes being sensitive, gentle, attractive, sexy, submissive, nurturing (as potential or actual mothers), emotional, and so on. We may still know nothing of the person of the woman—her real "self"—instead, we tend to judge and respond to how well she fits this socially prescribed image of femininity.

As if gender is supposed to make us so different, boys and men, by contrast, are supposed to be strong, competitive, dominant, intelligent, enterprising, rational, tough, determined, unemotional, and in control. Too many young men grow up believing this myth.

> A man is someone who doesn't show his feelings. He is hard and strong. My dad never showed his feelings, and he made sure I didn't either. "You've just got to get strong if you're ever going to be a man," he said. Yeah! He's a real asshole, my old man, but he can't fight 'cause he's a wimp!
>
> (Denver, 21)

Again, these attributes tell us little of the person of the man. It is as though a man hides behind a mask of masculinity, safe from emotional assaults against his true self.

men's denial of their emotional selves

There is a big price to pay for our conformity to these rigid social images: our real selfhood. For men, that means we try to disown, deny, or bury those parts of our human nature that don't fit, or directly conflict with, socially acceptable images of masculinity. Our emotional lives become the first and greatest casualties of our socialization as men—especially when it comes to the so-called "feminine" parts of our human nature. It is our socialization as men that is responsible for that disowning, that denial of our emotional selves. It is as though, for many of us, our socialization has been a kind of unrecognized, unintended assault upon the self, a sort of lifelong imposition of the demands of social image over the pursuit of true selfhood.

The tragedy is that we seem willing to impose those same demands upon ourselves throughout our adulthood. Then we recycle them, as it were, upon the lives of our children, and so the cycle of men's anger takes another turn: another generation of men's anger, another generation of assaulted selves.

what some men say about their anger

That's the theory of the origins of men's anger. Now let us hear what some other men say about themselves and their anger—and what their anger is saying about them. Notice especially how their anger covers so much of their personal pain and fear. You can sense in these extracts the lifetimes of emotional assaults upon these men's selfhoods. You can imagine how those assaults have formed a barrier to each man's struggle to become his true self.

> I live on a line between two fields: One's all milk and honey, the other's all rock and shit.
>
> I want to be on the good side of the line, but I have to live on a razor's edge—in the middle.
>
> Mom always said I deserved the bad side, and now I really feel guilty when I'm on the good side. I live it up fast on the good side until it blows up and I fall down again...on the bad side...and angry! (Jim, 36)
>
> I am a "fixer"—always have been, even as a kid. I fixed everything for everyone in the family—including the

in-laws. Dad died when I was still a kid. I couldn't save him—I failed! I swore I would never fail again! I am a man—a fixer.

Well, I was, until I injured my back at work. None of you can fix the pain, and soon I won't be able to work at all; that's what scares the shit out of me! If I can't work, who's going to look after my family? I won't be much of a fixer then. I'll be bloody dead! (Gary, 37)

Dad always said I have to be a man. Grandma died of breast cancer when she was 50 something and I was 9. Mom and Dad said Grandpa was to blame for neglecting her; now he's just wasting his life, wanting to die too.

Mom has lumps in her breast, too; she has migraines all day and is under emotional strain and fear. My job is to look after Mom and to keep the other kids from upsetting her. That's the rule—"Don't upset Mom." So I must keep all my emotions under control—especially my anger. Look what happened to Grandma when Grandpa neglected her; that's what will happen to Mom if I fail. Like Dad said: I've got to be a man about this! (Aaron, 21)

I'm one of the two bastards in our family; the other one's my father. "All men really are bastards," according to Mother! Who could blame her, the way *he* was?

When I succeeded at anything, as a kid, it was kind of, "So what? You're going to be a man. What do you want, a medal?" When I failed, Mother would support and care for me. So I failed . . . and kept failing.

As a young man, I became useless and unworthy. And I still am! The worst part is I can't even be angry, or I'll prove their point: that I really am an awful bastard.

(Rupert, 35)

I've allowed my height to dominate me. I'm too short, so I have to keep proving myself. (Doran, 49)

You won't recognize yourself in all these men; you might not see yourself in any. But can you hear any familiar words there? Is there any sense that what went on for even one of these men reminds you of any emotional experience in your life and your anger?

"Be a man; be strong; take control of life—even if you fail. But don't show your true feelings—especially your pain and fear!" That was (still is) the message for many men. It has also been the greatest assault of all upon their young male "selves."

the facts about men's anger

Let me present three facts to you about anger:

- Anger is a normal human emotion. It is part of the human condition all over the world.

- Anger is a problem when it produces violent behavior, when it threatens harm or damage, or when it affects your life or the lives of those around you. Anger is a problem, in other words, when it assaults your own or someone else's selfhood, health, and safety—physically or emotionally.

- For more and more people in our society today, men's anger is a problem.

male anger, female anger

"What about women?" you ask. "They are people too, and they get angry!"

True enough! But for women, anger is often different. There is still a strong cultural and gender bias that leaves many women feeling unentitled, prohibited from expressing anger, while many of those who do express it feel intimidated, put down, punished for being angry.[10] In my work, more women seek help with depression and guilt than with anger, but it often turns out that they have actually bottled up years of anger that they feel guilty for feeling! Ask any woman close to you what that's about, and she might tell you.

More obviously, anger does not as easily move so many women to violence as it seems to move so many men.

For men, there is a sense that it is okay for us to be angry—or at least that our anger is expected. The problem is that our anger often gets fuelled by all the unexpressed pain and unresolved fears of a lifetime—pain and fear that "real men" control, bury, or put aside in the interests of being a "man" and getting done what a "man" must get done. Yes, we need to face that too: the way our anger in one situation becomes a dangerous vehicle for the expression of emotional assaults upon our selfhoods that occurred in another time, another place.

> It's like an ugly beast inside me. I start to sound and look like my dad when he abused Mom and us kids. It's a loathing thing—self-loathing, you know. I was so angry at him for being so violent to us, and so angry at Mom for not leaving him and stopping the abuse. Now, when I feel attacked, stupid, like I'm not a man—I'm nothing; I just hate, you know, and I want to damage and hurt. Then I lose it and become "the ugly" and I just lash out. The worst part is I get to be just like him—an asshole.   (Kevin)

We'll explore that problem in more depth later, and create some solutions.

If you are a man who has a problem with anger, you are not alone; you are in company with millions of men at home and around the world. For many of us, anger is a problem to which the risk of violence is attached. Women who live with such men know the problem and the risk only too well.

solving your anger problem

To solve your anger problem, you first have to own it as part of your own emotional experience—it is not what someone else makes you feel. The good news is you can solve your anger problem—not by berating yourself as sick or sinful, but by recognizing yourself as a human being with an emotional life experience as well as a rational one. You are going to have feelings anyway, whether you ignore them, put them down, or hope they just go away—whether, in a word, you disown them. So isn't it better to own them, deal with the painful and fearful ones, and heal them? Or would you rather just keep them all tucked away down there until they explode again in your next angry rage? Come on! We are men, you and I. Healing the pain and confronting the fear that drives our anger are just two more challenges for us to overcome.

To succeed we had better get clear about what anger actually is.

how we experience anger...emotionally

We *experience* anger as an emotional feeling, not as a thought or an action. We feel angry in response to some internal or external event or experience that we perceive as an assault or threat of some kind. How we *express* our anger is something else altogether.

To reiterate, then, anger is an intense emotional experience; it is what we *feel*, not what we do in reaction to what we feel.

> My anger is like an intense heat. There's a fire right down in the pit of my stomach—burning embers of white-hot heat underneath. I can feel it burning more fiercely as I get really angry. Then it just erupts inside my body—not just upwards, but outwards. I'm lost in rage by then. Look out when the shit starts to fly. (Fabian)

a responsive emotional experience

Many of us experience the intense emotion of anger as a response to feeling seriously assaulted either physically, emotionally, mentally, or spiritually. That assault might be upon ourselves or it might be upon some other person, group, class, or population. (I always feel a deep sense of anger at the perpetrators of massacres or serious crimes against children.) We might also experience anger when we sustain some accidental injury for which nobody else was responsible. Finally, we might feel angry at our loss of parents, spouse, children, relatives, friends, home, or property.

an expressive emotional experience

Through the experience of anger we can express our pain, our fear, and our sense of powerlessness. Sometimes anger expresses a present physical or emotional experience, sometimes an accumulation of stored emotional experience from the past, sometimes both. Anger is one culturally acceptable way of expressing those feelings of pain, fear, and powerlessness that are otherwise unacceptable in most popular ideas about manhood and masculinity. Whereas sadness, hurt, and fear are regarded as signs of weakness, anger has most often been associated with manliness and strength. Indeed, our sports codes tend to encourage men to "shirtfront" their opponents—to bring some aggression into the game to satisfy the fans. Yet off the field that same aggression is against the law.

For men, anger speaks the unspeakable:

I just lost it and let him have it—with both barrels!

Anger protects us from the unprotectable:

I don't usually get emotional, but I was so mad!

Anger even forgives us the unforgivable:

He wouldn't have touched her if she hadn't made him so angry.

But anger should never be confused with those disrespectful, damaging, intimidating, and violent things we sometimes *do* when we are angry. The distinction between anger and violence is so important, yet it is poorly understood. Again, anger is what I *experience*; violence is what I *might do*. Therefore, I need to understand and heal the pain and fear that drive my anger; I need to control my anger, unfuelled by past assaults, so it no longer controls me.

so what is anger?

> Anger. It's a furnace of fire inside me. It just gets hotter and hotter the more fuel they—I—put on it. And then it just roars up from deep inside me, and that's it! I'm gone after that. (Mathew, 22)

Anger is an intense emotional experience. That's it! When I feel angry, that's all the truth there is: I feel angry.

Our challenge is not really to work *against* our anger, but to become aware of where it comes from, to take control of our anger and direct what we do with it. So now we need to ask, "What do men get angry at?" Or, perhaps more to the point, "*Whom* do we get angry at, most of all?"

That is what we are going to examine next.

chapter three

what do men get angry at?

I was angry with my friend; I told my wrath,
my wrath did end.
I was angry with my foe: I told it not,
my wrath did grow.

— William Blake[1]

Men get angry at all sorts of things. Mostly we get angry at ourselves. We get angry when we cannot do what we are supposed to do as "men" and when things get in our way. We get angry when we are frustrated, opposed, or seriously challenged. And we certainly get angry when we are ridiculed. We get angry when somebody hits us and when somebody cheats us. We get angry when we cannot perform: in bed, on the stage, at work, on the sports field. We get angry when we are physically hurt, too—ever been there when a man hits the wrong nail with his hammer? Most of all, we get angry when we cannot control what is happening to us. And when we get angry, we sometimes feel as if we lose control of what we are doing to others and ourselves.[2]

anger: do you lose it or use it?

Do you lose control of yourself when you get angry, or

do you get angry to gain control over others? Let's deal with that question up front.

The argument that anger is about losing control gets a lot of support in everyday language and in the ways we express our experience of our everyday relationships. "He lost his temper," "flew off the handle," "went berserk," "went ape-shit," "lost his cool" are all expressions that reflect the idea that to get angry is to lose control. I know myself, and I have been around and worked with a lot of men in my time, so I know how true this is. From my work with men, I also know that when they deal with and learn to control their anger, they do not get angry nearly so often, to nearly such an extent. As a result, these men stop their violent behavior altogether. You will read about some of them, and you will see for yourself as you work through this book alone or with a counselor. So anger certainly is most often and most disturbingly about losing control. But that's not the whole story.

Remember how in Chapter 1 I asked you to read and think about whether or not this book was right for you right now? I said that for men who *choose* to use violence as a means of enforcing their power and control over women, children, and others, this book on its own wouldn't provide all the help they required—they needed first to deal with their attitude of entitlement. I discussed how anger can be used as a form of coercion or violence to enforce my will or get my way, especially if I want to shut someone up or get her to do something out of fear of my anger. Have you ever used a line like one of the following with your partner or child?

"If you don't want me to blow up you'd better hold your tongue!"; "I've fuckin' had it with you. If you don't just do what I told you right now, I'm gonna lose my fuckin' temper and then the shit is really gonna fly around here!!!"

Here's how Dale puts it:

Fail or fight! That's what my life is about. As a kid growing up, my job was to protect other kids. That's who I am: a fighter for others, a protector. Problem was, I was never big, didn't do sports or martial arts.

But I learned real early that my anger was a huge source of energy. Then I discovered that other kids and men were intimidated by my rage. That was pretty cool, because often I never had to fight at all. I just let my anger do it for me.

(Dale, 28)

So, anger—or at least a good imitation of anger—can indeed be used as a tool of violence. If you choose to use anger in this way, you are really using a form of strategic violence; you need to go back to Chapter 1, "Man to Man," and get help to deal with your attitude.

For most men, however, anger is not about *control*, but about *losing control*.[3] From earliest childhood we learn that we will be judged as men by our ability to perform, provide, and protect. To succeed in these tasks, we quickly learn that we must control all those emotional features of our human nature that might threaten our success. The price we men pay for the level of control expected of us is our humanity...or at least those emotional parts of our humanity which, if we allow them in, seem to get so much in our way.

For most men, losing control is painful and fearful. We feel vulnerable, we judge ourselves, and we feel we have failed. We fear the consequences of losing control more than just about anything else. The pain of failure and the fear of losing control drive much of our anger.

climbing the scales of men's anger

The experience of anger can range for all of us from the trivial to the terrifying. While we take a look at some examples on that range or scale, try to identify which, if any, have elements you recognize from your experience of your own anger or the anger of someone you have known.

- Lowest on the anger scale might be the everyday experience of being annoyed at something that gets in your way or diverts you from your routine, like that flat tire when you are already five minutes late leaving for work. So you kick the paneling, hard. Then you kick it again and again until you exhaust your energy. Now, as well as needing to get the tire repaired, you have some badly dented paneling.

- A little higher, but still relatively low on the scale, is the anger you feel when someone intrudes on you. Someone just butts into whatever you are doing and assumes that the only proper concern you should have at that moment is with whatever is on his mind, whereas you have not the slightest interest in it. So you slam your hands on the desk and issue a few expletives before pointing to the door. Of course, there will be a complaint and your performance appraisal won't look quite so good—but what the hell!

- Higher still might be the powerless anger that bubbles up when the boss announces that your job has just been restructured out. But you have to control yourself—what's left of your "self"—so that you don't risk the best possible terms of any severance package you might be able to negotiate.

- Now let's go to the higher end of the anger scale. Have you ever had one of those really cruel emotional bouts with your partner, one that leaves nothing you can do or say to recover any ground between you? You can't seem to recapture your self-image as a man, nor struggle out of that deep pit of self-condemnation. Maybe you ranted and raved—shouting every obscenity you knew. Or, did you start throwing and breaking things? Did you kick the dog, the cat, the door? Maybe you smashed your fist through a wall or a window.

- Higher still, for some men, is when it's her you hit—first a controlling backhander, then a rib-shattering, full-bodied punch. You shove her screaming to the floor and yell at the kids to get back to their beds. It's so destructive, so full of harm, so violently out of control. Now you really feel like an "asshole."

- Finally, at the extreme, brutal, and tragic end of the scale comes the murderously disturbed anger of a respected but socially isolated cabinetmaker who lived in the Australian state of Tasmania. In June 1997, in bitter response to his perceived treatment by a world that seemed to him so inhuman, unfair, and corrupt, he slaughtered his four daughters so they could not live in it, axed off the hand that cut their throats, and with his remaining hand shot himself dead. Here was not power and control; here was bitter desperation and brutal defeat. Where once lived intimacy between father and children, there now reigned bloody savagery and violent death.

Unless you are in prison, the last example will be well outside your experience, thank God. But have you ever sensed in yourself elements of that cabinetmaker's view of the world?

All the examples I have just given, examples ranging between the lowest and highest extremes of anger, happen daily around our world. If we get angry enough, all of us are capable of some physical or emotional violence.

your anger is your responsibility

As men, most of us abhor the serious consequences of violence. Indeed, we are critical of any other man who reacts violently, especially to women and children—it's outside our code of honor, isn't it? I guess that is why we welcome any legal, social, psychological, or psychiatric explanations for extreme anger and violence. We feel safe in our self-assurance that such violence is not us—some psycho, deviant, or criminal maybe, but definitely not us. You know how it goes: "He must have been sick"; "What an asshole"; "I heard he was psychotic"; "Always knew there was something wrong with him"; "Didn't he have posttraumatic stress disorder?" No doubt you have responded to reports of violence by others in similar ways.

If only it were that simple, but unfortunately it is not. In extreme anger we all are capable of emotional or physical harm or damage. That is why it is so important for all of us—especially us men—to take personal responsibility for our own anger so that it cannot turn to violence.

defuelling your anger—from the inside

Taking on the responsibility for our anger involves a process of internal emotional healing. Ironically, to defuel our anger, we need to know less about who or what we get angry at (the objects of our anger) and more about where inside ourselves it comes from (the subjects of our anger). We need to get to know and deal with the internal, emotional sources of our anger. We cannot really do much to change the people or events we get angry at; we can only do something to change ourselves and what we do about those people or events. And that is what anger defuelling is—a process of internal change.

Thus, my objective with men who come to me for help with their anger is to start the process of internal change and restore access to all of their selves—their emotional and experiential selves as well as their rational and intellectual selves.[4] We start by revisiting those earliest assaults upon the self, those first experiences of intense anger, so often deriving from our earliest experiences of pain, fear, and powerlessness.

stories of healing and changing

First, let us look at three men who have known different levels of trauma in their lives: Terry, Rajid, and Peter (not their real names). Their stories are not exceptional, in my experience, but they might be different from your own. Even so, these men's stories illustrate the link between fear and pain and anger—with some of its consequences. They might also hint at how the process of owning and restoring—or "restorying"—their emotions started the process of healing. I hope they will help start the same process for you.

terry's story

Terry was angry at his family of origin and his childhood. Especially he was angry at his father, who killed himself brutally with a shotgun when Terry was 18 months old. Terry was not told until he was 26 that it was he whom his mother sent out as a toddler to find his father's body in the backyard. Terry's mother then acquired a succession of inept and dependent partners while Terry was required to grow up as the family fixer, the problem solver—the "man" of the house. Seeking comfort and fathering, Terry "found God" in a revivalist church. He also found there the woman he soon married. She had two children from a previous and violent marriage. To add to the challenges of their marriage, she was morphine-dependent for relief of pain from a deteriorating postsurgical bowel disorder.

Terry was to be caring, supportive, and Christian in all that he did. To express his anger and outrage was not only distressing for his wife, it was sinful before their God. Not only were Terry's pain and fear to be silenced, so also was his only learned "manly" means of expressing them—through his anger. He kept the lid on his anger as much as he could, but it broke out under stress. In his rage Terry would abuse God and his wife in emotional, fear-filled episodes. His wife sent Terry to their pastor.

Terry's pastor's counseling was based on faith, hope, charity, and dutiful trust in the Lord. Therefore, all had to be forgiven—his father, his mother, her men, and his brutalized childhood—without his pain or fear or powerlessness ever being heard or acknowledged. It did not work; things became worse for Terry, his wife, their marriage, and her children. Terry became depressed and was put on medication. He was referred to me by an alert and sensitive physician.

We sourced Terry's original anger to his brutalized childhood and the dispossessing assaults upon his selfhood. Terry expressed his pain and fear; I heard, shared, and honored them as valid parts of his emotional experience as a human being and as a man. Old demons were laid to rest, and we made progress with his anger. You'll meet Terry again—a happier, healthier, and more effective man—in Chapter 14.

rajid's story

Rajid described himself as paranoid. He had good reason to be. A former dealer in the Sydney drug scene, Rajid was about to give evidence that would convict the perpetrator of a violent murder. He barricaded himself in his home and slept with a hammer under his pillow. He desperately wanted out of "the scene" and to put his life back on a stable and legal footing— but his background and his enemies made it so hard. Rajid had fallen into dealing as the logical occupational choice of some- one who had learned since childhood that the only way to pro- tect yourself was to coerce and control others by force. But his angry outbursts were getting worse—more frequent and out of control. He didn't know where it all came from, but it scared him more and more each day. His physician referred him to me for management of his anger and anxiety.

The astonishing thing about Rajid was his sensitivity to and obvious care for his girlfriend, their child, and another on the way. It seemed out of character for a tough guy from the underworld whose iron rule since prep school had been "don't get scared; get control!" Rajid's rule was harsher than the usual manhood rule about not *showing* fear; it demanded that he not let himself *experience* fear under any circumstance. I wondered what kind of life of dispossessing assaults upon the self could have produced such a rigid rule in a man. I soon found out.

Rajid's childhood, youth, and early adulthood were not those found in heaven. He had a history of expulsions from school, solitary confinements in prison, and warfare with police and rival gangs. And it all started in his sister's closet with a common childhood prank that went horribly wrong. At age six or seven, Rajid had sleepwalked into the closet and, while still asleep, urinated all over his feet. Presumably because his sister had found him there and called their brother to share the joke, the brother had locked Rajid inside while he was still asleep. He awoke eventually to the smell of his urine-soaked feet and the pitch black of his confinement. Unable to escape, Rajid panicked. When he was finally released in shock, terror, and tears, he remembered well the family rule that "you didn't tell"—not parent or anyone else. This rule was part of growing up to be a man. From then on, Rajid's brother and sister enticed him into the closet many times on all sorts of pretexts. When that no longer worked, they used coercion. For several years this childish prank went on, years in which Rajid learned the rule he was to live by: "don't get scared, get control."

In therapy we dealt not with Rajid's violence but with his fear, which previously could never be expressed—not since the closet incidents.[5] Until he was referred for therapy, Rajid's life had become an all-pervasive mission to get out or stay out of the closet, the driving force of his anger. The more determined he became, the more violence he committed, and the more he got locked up. Rajid had traded his sister's closet for a jail cell. Once he dealt with the pain and fear-filled memories of those dispossessing assaults on his selfhood, Rajid got better. He was able to reintegrate his emotional self: to own his pain and fear as well as his joy, his weakness as well as his strength, his grief as well as his love. His anger subsided; he and his girlfriend and their children now had some peace and stability in their lives. You will see quite a lot of Rajid later in the book.

peter's story

Peter was twenty-three when he was referred to me for management of his underlying anger and violent episodes. He had previously been diagnosed and treated for depression, and a hospital emergency center had referred him to me. Brought up in an Eastern European family in which respect for male authority was exacted without question, Peter found his marriage collapsing as his wife withheld that respect in favor of her own selfhood and her frustrated attempts to be her "own person" within the marriage. It seemed to Peter that her family was colonizing him into their Australian family culture and values, both quite foreign to him. The more he tried to counter their influence, the more his wife withdrew and went out on her own, and the more angry and depressed Peter became. The couple separated, and the focus of their conflict turned to their home, property, and other assets. Peter, fearing he would lose everything, fell deeper into depression and was taken by his mother to the emergency room.

It sounded like the fairly common story of a failed marriage—until I asked Peter what in his early life hurt him so badly to make him so angry. Three episodes stood out in his memory.

At the age of eight or nine, Peter was playing rough at school and accidentally broke his friend's arm. The school reported the incident to Peter's father, who beat him up.

At the age of ten, Peter was at soccer practice when his father's parents visited unexpectedly for dinner. They ate without him, leaving nothing for the boy when he arrived home. Instead, his father beat him mercilessly for being late.

At the age of thirteen, Peter was holding a light for his father to do a repair job at night. The job went wrong, and his father blamed Peter for not holding the light right. He physically kicked him all over the house, bruising him badly and drawing blood from a head wound.

The most enduring picture Peter had of his childhood was of his angry and violent father abusing the whole family.

There was little enough chance of any lasting reconciliation between Peter and his estranged wife, not after all the anger he'd thrown at her—anger he really needed to express to his father and about his misguided ideas of manhood. There was no chance at all as long as the whole conflict was conducted as a tug of war over property. Yet, in Peter's tradition of manhood, it was humiliating enough to be unable to hang on to your wife; to lose your home and property was the ultimate shame.

Clearly, Peter's anger was being driven largely by the chronic pain of all those assaults on his selfhood as a child and by his overpowering fear of loss as a man. Anger was the only emotion available to him. For a "real man" to express pain and fear openly and honestly was unacceptable. Doing so in therapy was the first time Peter had done so since he learned the "rules of manhood" at around age eight. That's when Peter was able to drop his end of the tug of war and start to get on with his life.

You can see how anger came to run the lives of these three men. "What would you expect?" I hear you ask. "Weren't all of their early lives marked by violence, abuse, or trauma?" And, of course, you are right.

Now let us consider the more typical story of an angry man who had never known violence in his life, had never been abused or ever experienced any unusual trauma. Let us see if I can unearth for you the pain and fear that was no less real, no less difficult for him, no less present as the driving force of his anger.

patrick's story

Patrick, age forty-one, was a fencing contractor from Western Australia. He was married with two children. Patrick had won a major contract in Victoria, so he stayed there during the week and flew home on weekends. He had been getting seriously angry and yelling at his wife, Jane, in front of her friends (never *his* friends) whenever they were out for an evening in Perth or away together on camping trips with their families.

The problem had started some years earlier—soon after Jane had graduated from the university with a science degree. Until then, she had been a nursing aide at a local hospital. Soon after she graduated, Jane was snapped up by a commercial laboratory and embarked upon a promising career. Her friends were fellow graduates and professional colleagues. They all seemed to know so much more than Patrick, always acted "right" when he felt they judged him to be wrong, ill-informed, and ignorant. They all seemed so superior and better educated that Patrick just couldn't reach them. And so he reacted, becoming verbally aggressive, with put-downs, insults, and the like—always to Jane, never to her friends.

Jane frequently began to feel her self-esteem being dragged down. She did not need this, and she was not going to tolerate it anymore. She demanded that Patrick do something about his anger or she was going to leave! Patrick felt defensive, threatened, and guilty—which only served to escalate and intensify his anger towards Jane. That was when he came to me.

Patrick's early life seems to have been so uneventful that he recalls nothing of his childhood before he left school to work with his father in the fencing business. He does remember two overall themes. One, his relationship with his father was based only on football and fencing; two, his relationship with his mother was based on "equity." She cared for the family—Dad, Patrick, and his sister Casey—and controlled their relationships on the basis that everyone was treated equally and "the same" in all things.

Dad ran the business and never consulted or shared anything about that with his wife. Mom ran the family and never consulted or shared anything about that with her husband. There was never any open conflict expressed between them since their division of labor and responsibilities was clear, understood by all, and never challenged. The only mild disagreement that occurred was over whether or not Patrick should finish high school. Mom thought he should, while Dad thought he should drop out and enter the business with him. Patrick just assumed that leaving school was what he would, should, and wanted to do. So that was what he did, and all was resolved.

Patrick didn't really know then how it all worked out for Casey; he is only really getting to know her well now. But basically, under Mom's law of equity, no one was to be any different from anyone else—that would not have been fair. Patrick grew closer and closer to his father in all things—so much that there was a real and practical sense in which they became no different; what his dad was, so was Patrick. Patrick grew up with almost no sense of who he was himself. Life was divided into two distinct streams—work and home. Dad worked and Mom ran the home. So when Patrick got married, Patrick worked and Jane ran the home—simple as that. Except it wasn't to be quite that simple.

Patrick's parents began to fight with each other once his sister, and then he, left home. Confronted with each other and with no children to filter things through, their old unspoken and unresolved conflicts began to emerge. One of these stood out. It had always been assumed that Patrick would take over his dad's fencing business . . . until his mom came in with the issue of equity!

As far as Mom was concerned, if Patrick was to have the business, he would have to share it equally with his sister. Not that Casey wanted it, but that's how things were done in their family under Mom's equity rule. The question remained unresolved for fifteen years; Patrick buttoned his lip as he had always done and as his father before him had always done. He became increasingly fearful for the future security of his own new family, but he had neither the confidence nor the perceived right to say anything.

There was another related handicap with which Patrick grew up: Men like him and his father did not express or share their personal, internal feelings, such as anger or fear or pain. Men bottled them up inside. A common enough experience for men in our society was made even more difficult for Patrick by the fact that feelings belong in the emotional zone and the concept of equity belongs in the rational zone. He just couldn't raise anger against equity—it wasn't fair or reasonable—and, anyway, equity was right and proper, inarguable.

Patrick never realized how increasingly angry he had become until Jane had made her recent stand and demanded he do something about it. But he did realize how intolerant he had grown of his mother's quibbling and how he resented more and more the time he had to spend with her on his visits. He did not understand why or how his intolerance and resentment had come about until he discovered, in therapy, how angry he was at her. Instead of expressing his anger at his mother, he would wait until he got home or, if Jane were with him, until they got into the car. Then, having stewed on his anger for a while, he would take it out on Jane.

Now Patrick started to understand how his anger at Jane's "educated" friends—again taken out on her, not them, although in front of them—was really anger at himself. So insecure, lacking in confidence, and incompetent did he feel about himself that Jane's friends were touching his anger buttons—his sense of not being a worthwhile and unique person in his own right.

Patrick's anger healing had to begin with his mother, not his wife. This was his responsibility, not hers. But his mother was getting old, and he felt he didn't have the right to "hurt" her. The challenge he faced was this: how to confront his mother's equity rule without hurting her, after all these years and when she was now old and frail. While trying to deal with this problem in therapy, Patrick discovered there was something else his anger had gotten in the way of him telling his mother, and that was how much he had loved her and still did. But because of his family's rigid rules against overt displays of emotion, he couldn't do this either. So, he did the only thing he could; he told his wife, Jane. For 3½ hours they really talked and listened and shared, and for the first time since they married twenty years earlier, Patrick opened up to Jane about his emotional life. Then he went and collected his mom and took her out for afternoon tea—with Jane. Without words, Patrick showed his mom—and himself—how you could be different and equal at the same time. He has not had a serious anger episode since!

There were other, secondary gains as well. Patrick learned to own and express his feelings effectively with the right people at the right times. He is now able to be physically and emotionally close and giving to his own children. They in turn have responded to him with childish warmth, trust, and love. Their early childhood behavior problems have settled down as Patrick takes a much more active but relaxed and intimate role in their lives.

Finally, Patrick, Jane, and their children have spent a recent long weekend with some of those friends of Jane, the same ones he once saw as superior and better educated. Guess what? They all had a ball! Patrick was relaxed; he did not even need to invoke the practical anger-avoidance strategies we had rehearsed in therapy, and he just didn't feel angry. It has been that way ever since.

what emotional fuel drives your anger?

We just saw how anger came to run the lives of four ordinary men. It is not too different from the way anger came to run my life for many years and how anger runs (or ruins) the lives of many men and the lives of those close to them.

- For Terry, it was his father's violent suicide and his mother's childlike dependency that left him carrying the pain and fear that drove his adult anger.

- For Rajid, it was a prolonged childhood prank turned traumatically violent and a family governed by the "don't tell" rule.

- For Peter, it was years of physical and emotional abuse of himself, his mother, and his sisters by a violent father.

- For Patrick, it was an uneventful, "normal" family life in which Dad took care of business and Mom took care of home, but where an otherwise laudable equity was enforced above all other needs and considerations.

For me, it was the extremes of 1950s Catholic culture within a social class system. The first "fact of life" I learned was enshrined in the prayer we had drummed into us before we could receive our First Communion: "Lord, I am not worthy. . . ."

So what was it for you? What was it in your transition from childhood to manhood that fuelled the fires of your anger? You might not be able to answer that right now, but you will in the next few chapters.

how we assault ourselves

Whatever incidents fuelled your fires of anger, those experiences constitute an accumulation of assaults upon the self.[6] Those assaults begin at an early age to alienate us from those parts of ourselves that would otherwise be available to us to experience. I am talking about our emotional selves: all that soft stuff around our experience of fear and sadness, hurt and weakness, uncertainty and insecurity, confusion and panic; all those human needs we have for security and joy, comfort and nurture, surety and safety, clarity and peace.

Those emotions exist unconsciously within our selves, though obstructed from recognition. We would like to cast them out like demons: embarrassments to us within the masculine subculture of our daily lives; suspect, deviant, perhaps immoral, but certainly unmanly in the parent culture of our society and its institutions. So we assault ourselves further with our efforts to put them down, keep them from discovery, hide them from public view. The protection of our public persona (our social image) is paramount. The cost of that protection is our alienation—from ourselves, from each other, and from the whole of who we are. But our self-alienation is also self-wounding and self-defeating: It assaults our selfhoods more painfully than any assault that would come from someone else. And so we get angry...especially at ourselves. Can you see that in your own life?

Our anger is both the expression of our alienation and our protection against exposure.

restoring your self

Indeed, anger is a complex and intense emotional experience. Yet, for many of us men, it has been the safest emotion there is! Why? Because our anger masks all that pain and fear that our manhood demands we must never reveal.

But at what terrible cost in fear and harm for the women and children around us, for our families and homes. This is a good place to go back and review your Anger Volatility Index in Chapter 1 (pages 28–36) and to assess one more time the actual risk your anger poses for your wife, partner or girlfriend, and children.

The anger-defuelling process involves, first, unmasking the pains and fears that drive our anger, and then re-owning them—instead of disowning and denying them as somehow unmanly. Then we can express them openly and resolve them effectively, for better emotional health. Although you and I cannot meet in person, I hope the following chapters will help you along the path to defuelling your anger and restoring the whole person you are inside. Again, if you think you might have trouble doing this on your own, get some help.

...first with
your heart...

discovering the source of your anger

A man travels the world in search of what he needs
And returns home to find it.

— George Moore[1]

So, what *does* make you so angry? If you could find the answer to that, you'd have your problem licked, right? And you'd give *anything* for that, wouldn't you? So get ready to give a lot—of yourself!

the big search

Some men might say women make them angry. Or the kids. Or the boss. Or the idiot in the car beside them at the traffic lights. Or the government. Or whatever. If only anger were that simple! You would be out of trouble and I would be out of work!

But it just is not that simple, is it? All those people and things and events that *trigger* your anger aren't going away, are they? And even if they do go away for a while, they keep coming back. That is the problem with anger for so many of us: it just keeps coming back. So until you find the source of your anger, it is most likely to keep coming back for you, too.

Looking for the source of your anger may be the biggest search of your life, but it is not one you will have to travel the world for. That is because the emotional secrets that drive your anger are all right there at home inside yourself. You still will need to be heroic in your search to uncover the secrets—some painful, some fear-filled—that will answer the question: "What *does* make me so angry?" But then at last you will be able to do something about it.

finding the source of your anger

As I have already said, it is much more helpful to understand anger as a normal, human, emotional response to what we perceive as an assault upon the self than it is to think of anger as a sin, psychosis, or maladaptive behavior. *Anger is an emotion, not a behavior or an action.* Here we are concerned with understanding the accumulation of other emotions, like pain and fear, that such assaults seem to generate, but to which many men seem able to respond *only with anger.*

Emphasizing the importance of understanding emotions is not to say that anger is not problematic. Clearly, it can become so, or you would not be reading this book. The question is, do you lay a guilt trip or a label on people who get angry? Or do you get creative and empower them to explore their own *internal resources* for the means to change how they experience the events and other people that trigger their anger? For me, the latter is a much more positive, constructive, and helpful way to go.

So how do you access those internal resources?

In Chapter 5, we are going to learn how to explore and rediscover our emotional experiences for the clues to what makes us so angry that we sometimes lose control and go over the top. We are going to source our anger back to those important emotional experiences of assaults upon the self.

In later chapters, we will learn how to identify and utilize all of our potential strengths and resources to manage our anger episodes in practical ways. These will include the physical, behavioral, and emotional signals to our anger, as well as the resources and opportunities that exist already in our immediate environments.

First, though, we need to know what we are looking for. Specifically, we are looking for the emotional experiences of our earlier life (from childhood, adolescence, and adulthood) that drive our present anger. Those emotional experiences are likely to be painful and fearful, and you might find it awkward and uncomfortable to revisit them. This should not surprise you, since you may have felt yourself seriously assaulted by some of those experiences. Ironically, the most difficult emotional experiences of your life will become your greatest resources for the challenging task of solving your anger problem.

finding your emotional resources

Some of the most important internal resources at our disposal for dealing with anger are our emotional resources. To access those internal resources, you will go on an expedition within yourself that takes you back through what I call your emotional biography.[2]

What will you look for on that expedition?

You will look for those emotional experiences that were painful or fearful and never properly owned and dealt with. You will search for the old demons that drive your anger today. These are the internal resources that—once you recognize and know how to use them—will defuel your anger and possibly change your life. They are also the sources of your anger; deal with the source, and you will deal with your anger.

what drives anger?

About 25 years ago, when I first started to ask serious questions about serious anger, I was frustrated by the biggest question of all: "What drives anger?"

I have pursued that question with all of my "angry" clients since then. I have found that those clients have kept presenting me with a common theme to their anger. The unexpressed, hidden, disowned, but accumulated experiences of pain and fear, associated with all of the assaults upon their "selves" these men felt they had endured, had become the demons that now drove their anger. As they opened themselves and began their struggle to deal with their demons—as they began to heal themselves—I noticed how dramatically their anger subsided. They were getting angry less often and less intensely. These men needed to separate out the emotions associated with events of the past so they could deal with emotions associated with events of the present. As the frequency and intensity of their anger decreased, the attendant risks of violence were eliminated.

reclaiming your emotional self

To start opening up, confronting these feelings, and dealing with them was always hard work for these men. It was work that seemed to demand of them enormous courage. It was as though they first had to break through all the unwritten rules and taboos about manhood and masculinity, to challenge for themselves what it meant to be a "man." Only then could they reclaim and repossess their human birthright to their emotional selves.

If that was true for me and for all the men with whom I have worked over the last couple of decades, then these mountains of manhood might be a challenge for you to conquer, too. If so, I would like to recommend another book to you. Every man I know who has read it (including me) has gained a heap of encouragement from it. The book is called *Manhood: An Action Plan for Changing Men's Lives.*[3] It is very popular in Australia and overseas. Steve Biddulph, the author, is an Australian who seems to have had struggles similar to yours and mine.

So, the bottom line for your anger problem is this: If you want to cool the fire of your anger, you first have to defuel it. The fuel for most men is their accumulated emotional pain and fear—usually kept tightly under wraps, tightly controlled and disowned. That is where you have to go to the source of your demons and deal with them.

a word of warning

The work you will be invited to do in Chapter 5 is emotionally demanding. For many, it will feel awkward; for none of you will it be comfortable. You will need to draw upon all of your reserves of courage and determination to succeed at your goal—to come to terms with the feelings that drive your anger.

a word about seeking outside help

You may find that the work in Chapter 5 brings up memories and feelings that you find too hard to deal with on your own. The support of a trusted friend or relative will help a lot—especially if you have someone you can freely open up to. A qualified and experienced professional counselor can also help you get past the rough times, encourage you to continue, and keep you focused upon your goal. You may well have a professional counselor, agency, clinic, or men's program near you. But please make sure whoever you consult has a copy of this book and has read it cover to cover, or agrees to keep up with your reading and work through the book with you.

and a word of encouragement

The rewards for your courage and determination are many and great. You might experience a new sense of peaceful self-acceptance. When you accept full responsibility for that which is yours—your pain, your fear, your anger—you will learn to punish and blame yourself much less. You will come to understand and like yourself a little more than you might have lately. You might even hold your head a little higher, your shoulders back a little further. Even if you feel saddened temporarily, you will experience a new sense of wholeness within yourself as you rediscover a bigger, more dignified, more honorable vision of your manhood—the real man within. You will also want to get into the next chapters of this book more eagerly—and indeed into the rest of your life—as you move from self-blame to self-responsibility and recognize the real possibilities for change.

the task and the challenge

The task is difficult; the reason for the task is simple: Until you can see what it is you need to deal with and change, you can do neither. By the end of your work in Chapter 5, you will see clearly enough; learning how to deal with it and make the changes you need to make will be comparatively easy as you continue through the rest of this book and your life.

So, now I ask you for a commitment: Are you up to the challenge, or not?

If you decide that you are not yet up to it, just put the book down and come back to it when you can. I know it will be tough going, but I also know what this process has done for my clients, myself, and the people we care about. Think about it . . . it's your life, and your anger!

If you decide that you are ready and are willing to give it your best shot, come with me on a journey of discovery that will lead you to the resources you need to start the process of healing your pain, challenging your fears, and calming your anger. It may well change your whole life.

So don't procrastinate; make a decision to commit or postpone. If you postpone, set a date now to review your decision or to book an appointment with a counselor to get you started.

the emotional bioscan for anger

It is not because things are difficult that we do not dare;
It is because we do not dare that they are difficult.

— *Seneca*[1]

Hello again. Either you are still here or you took a break and came back with your commitment to explore. So let's do it!

Anger is an intense, expressive, and responsive emotional experience. Therefore, the process for finding the source of your anger is a process of searching, recognizing, owning, and dealing with the emotional experiences that fuel or drive it.

your bioscan is your emotional biography[2]

Over recent years I have been developing, with my clients, a successful method of sourcing anger. It is especially helpful for men, although I use the same basic process for women. I call this process the Emotional BioScan for Anger, or BioScan for short. Your BioScan is your emotional biography. Just as each of us has our own biography—the story of our life—so we each have an emotional biography—the story of our emotional life.

your emotional bank account

Like a savings account, your emotional biography carries within it all of the long-forgotten emotional experiences of your life so far—all of its transactions, big and small, both the ones that feel good and the ones that don't feel so good. You deposit all of your emotional experiences into this account; thus, you keep adding to your emotional biography, much the same way you keep making deposits into your savings account. And, as with your savings account, you accumulate emotional interest on your balance.

emotional "deposits"

Into your emotional biography, you deposit several different kinds of emotional experiences. Basically, emotions fall into two types: the ones we want to have (happiness, joy, excitement, peace, etc.) and the ones we do not especially want to have (sadness, hurt, fear, anger, etc.). Some psychologists and other professionals categorize the first group as positive emotions and the second as negative emotions. The truth is, they are all very normal human emotions that for most of us go with the business of living. We would all like to do what we can to enjoy as much as possible of the one type and to avoid as much as possible of the other. Some of us find that fairly hard to do. Most of us try at least to maintain and grow an emotionally healthy balance in our biography, just as we try to maintain and grow a financially healthy balance in our savings account.

emotional "withdrawals"

With our emotional biography, as well as trying to maintain and grow the balance of "good" experiences, we also seem to need to keep eliminating all the "bad" experiences. Sadly, what most of us men learned to do in our youth was to sweep bad experiences under the carpet of our "manhood." So those painful and fearful experiences just stayed there, inside our emotional accounts, accruing "interest." They were seldom, if ever, withdrawn, except through anger.

By and large, we men just do not make effective withdrawals of pain or fear from our emotional accounts. So when I ask you to scan your emotional biographies for the pain and fear that drive your anger, I know very well that I am asking a very big thing!

taking the plunge

I would like you now to work through the Emotional BioScan for Anger—a seven-step process for discovering the source of your anger. What you do with the BioScan is track back through your emotional biography for all those major emotional deposits of pain and fear that you either consigned to your unconscious emotional memory or that you are conscious of and that have been eating away at you, but that you have never effectively owned and dealt with. At the end of this exercise comes the big revelation. You get to see quite clearly, perhaps for the first time ever, how the emotional baggage you've stored inside all this time affected your balance last time you got seriously angry.

Please take your time and read carefully through this chapter a couple of times before you start work on your own BioScan. For a few readers, this might not be the first time you have attempted to search your past for emotional memories. But for every reader, it will be the first time you have used your own anger as a window to your past and its memories. All of the seven steps are repeated in the "how-to" section and in the examples. The repetition should be helpful, but do take the time and care to learn.

the emotional bioscan for anger

---

step 1. Recall your last serious anger episode.

---

step 2. Recall the mental images that surfaced during this episode, but that might have come from previous experiences of perceived assaults upon your self.

---

step 3. Recall the emotional feelings you had during this episode that seemed more intense than the event itself and that might relate to those previous experiences.

---

step 4. Recall where, when, and with whom you have had those mental images or emotional feelings before this episode. Is there any sense of déjà vu?

---

step 5. Recall previously forgotten painful or fearful events or periods from anywhere in your life that were resurrected by this anger episode or by the review you are doing right now.

---

step 6. Review steps 2–5 of your BioScan, and identify those mental images, emotional feelings, déjà vu events, and previously forgotten painful or fearful events that you sense might have been driving your anger during the episode recalled in step 1.

---

step 7. Identify those issues of pain and fear you need to own and deal with to defuel your anger.

---

how to use the bioscan

Carefully read the seven steps a couple of times.

Read the section "Compiling Your BioScan" (below) and the rules that follow.

Then read the section "How to Complete the Seven Steps" (below), including the examples. The first is my own, under the heading "Frank's BioScan," and the second is Benjamin's, under the heading "Benjamin's BioScan."

Finally, read the section "The Emotional BioScan for Anger" (above) one more time to make sure you understand the steps involved. If you are still in doubt about any of the steps, review that step in the section "How to Complete the Seven Steps." You can also read again my BioScan, Benjamin's, or both.

When you've reread the seven steps and read both examples, you will be as well equipped as you can be. That's when you start writing your own BioScan.

compiling your bioscan

There are several ways of doing the BioScan:[3]

- You could write it as a letter to yourself or to someone else who is important to you. It will never be received by anyone except you, because it stays with you.

- You could write it as a short story or an essay.

- You could prepare it as a confidential report, with bullet points and/or headings before each paragraph.

- You could use pen and paper, typewriter, or your personal computer. Or, you could dictate the whole thing into a cassette recorder.

Whatever method you adopt and whatever medium you use, there are four basic rules you must establish for yourself before you start.

basic rules

1. Try to listen and pay attention to your gut feelings—however painful they may be—*not* to your head's thinking. It is your emotional ability to feel that you need to explore, not your intellectual ability to rationalize or explain.

2. Don't worry about spelling and grammar—just aim for a smooth flow, a buildup of momentum.

3. Give yourself enough space, but don't go overboard. One page is unlikely to be enough to accommodate your entire emotional biography; on the other hand, ten pages is probably too much to deal with well.

4. Your record must be secured where no one else will find it and read it—unless you want them to—no matter how close such a person might be to you. This is your emotional biography we are dealing with here, and you must feel safe about it. Treat it as though your own life or someone else's depends on it. In many ways, it does!

how to complete the seven steps

Step 1. Recall your last serious anger episode.

Try to relive the experience of your last serious anger episode in your mind and in your gut.

- What happened? Who or what was involved?

- Did you find out your partner had been unfaithful sexually or in some other way?

- Had you been confronted or caught with something you yourself had done wrong?

- Was it an argument that got out of hand, about the children maybe?

- Was it a task you were trying to do but couldn't, or one that went wrong for you?

- Were you being accused of something? Blamed for something?

- Were you attacked physically or emotionally, or being victimized in some way?

- Had something happened to you, your partner or family, your coworkers, or friends?

- What did you actually do in reaction to this event and your anger?

- What was/were the outcome/s—for yourself and/or for others?

- Were you just angry with yourself and/or the world in general?

Your last serious anger episode could have been about one or more of these, or a dozen other things. It is important to be clear about the events that led to and occurred during your episode.

Step 2. Recall the mental images that surfaced during this episode, but that might have come from previous experiences of perceived assaults upon your self.

What I mean by "mental images" are all the mental pictures of yourself and others, the way things sounded to you, and the feelings you had at that time—especially feelings of pain or fear. I'm asking you to remember all those internal experiences that came to your awareness when you were angry. Try to identify any of those internal experiences that (either at the time or in hindsight) seem to have come up before in your life. You might have experienced them in previous, unrelated situations; you might have experienced them last month, last year, ten years ago, back in your teens, or in your childhood. These internal experiences might have come up several times during your life.

A helpful hint here is to remember what you or the other parties involved (your spouse, children, friend, boss, etc.) said or did, just before or when you got really angry, that triggered that internal response or "kick" within you. Then, before it goes away again or slips from your mind, record that internal response—not what the other person said or did and not what you said or did, but *what you saw or experienced inside yourself in response.*

Step 3. Recall the emotional feelings you had during this episode that seemed more intense than the event itself and might relate to those previous experiences.

Be aware of any feelings you had of venom, hatred, revenge, or hostility that seem now to have been exaggerated or somehow over-the-top. Try to identify any feelings that came up for you during your anger episode that did not quite fit the events or the people you were angry with at the time.

A helpful hint here is to ask this question: "In hindsight, did that person or thing collect from me more than his/her/its fair share of my anger at the time?"

Step 4. Recall where, when, and with whom you have had those mental images or emotional feelings before this episode. Is there any sense of déjà vu?

Recall any sense of déjà vu that came up during your last episode or now while you are reconstructing it. By "déjà vu," I mean a kind of sixth-sense awareness you get sometimes, when you find yourself saying, "Hey! I've been here before," or, "I've experienced something like this somewhere else in my life."

Scan the last ten years, the decade before that, the one before that, and so on, back to early childhood. Or, you can scan periods defined by "landmarks," such as marriages, births of children, job starts and finishes, teenage years, high school and primary school days, childhood at home, the birth of siblings, and so on.

Who was involved? What were the events and their outcomes for you?

What did you or others do about them? Was it a one-time event? Was it repeated a few times or often? Was it just the way things always were for you at that time?

Step 5. Recall previously forgotten painful or fearful events or periods from anywhere in your life that were resurrected by this anger episode or by the review you are doing right now.

Pay special attention to and record any emotionally or physically traumatic events that generated similar emotional pain or fear that you have never been able to express or reveal.

Step 6. Review steps 2–5 of your BioScan, and identify those mental images, emotional feelings, déjà vu events, and previously forgotten painful or fearful events that you sense might have been driving your anger during the episode recalled in step 1.

If you imagine your last anger episode as a boiler, then you are searching for all the emotional fuel firing the furnace below it—not just the latest fuel (i.e., the events that triggered your last anger episode), but all the hot coals beneath it that heated and fired that latest fuel.

Step 7. Identify those issues of pain and fear you need to own and deal with to defuel your anger.

This is the most important step of the BioScan, recognizing and owning all those issues of pain and fear that were never dealt with properly. Long stored in your unconscious, but unavailable to you until now, these are the issues you need to resolve to take the heat out of your anger. For most men in counseling, the issues tend to emerge from step 6.

You will see what I mean when you get to steps 6 and 7 in the BioScans for me and Benjamin.

As you read these two examples, be alert to any signals of recognition: anything that Benjamin or I have to say about our emotional biographies that might trigger something in your own. Jot down on paper any familiar feelings or memories you become aware of as you read.

frank's bioscan

Step 1. Recall your last serious anger episode.
We've had our two closest friends, Patrick and Parena, from the city up to our home in Mt. Macedon. They've brought with them their friend Simon, who's visiting from California. We've all been hiking, and I've cooked a barbecue dinner on our front deck. It's an idyllic setting, with views across the lowlands to Melbourne in the east and the Wombat Ranges in the southwest. We've finished a few bottles of wine between us, and we're enjoying a glass of port in the late summer evening.

We're asking Simon about his family's business in the United States, and the talk turns to the American and Australian economies and politics. Simon boasts a recently posted U.S. unemployment rate of just 4 percent. I challenge that figure and charge that, as in Australia, the unemployment rates that governments advertise are couched in terms that never reveal anything like the true unemployment picture. An argument develops—mostly between us men—about social, racial, political, and ideological issues around what I see as the deepening economic crisis internationally and its impact upon working-class people and the poor in our two countries.

The whole debate gets way out of hand as all three of us defend our positions and lose track of the emotional heat that's building between us. Patrick gets angry, partly due (as I learn the next day) to his growing embarrassment and hurt that their American friend is being criticized when he should be receiving our hospitality as a guest. I get angry at Patrick, as his extreme right-wing views (as I see them) challenge my own left-wing social, political, and personal values.

As I get more and more angry, I start verbally attacking Patrick, very personally. I lose my temper, throw my glass over our veranda rail to the driveway below, and storm off to cool down. I'm well past my threshold, and I'm doing the only nonviolent thing left to me: I escape.

While I'm out walking down my anger energy level, Patrick, Parena, and Simon get in their car and leave. When I return, Anne is deeply hurt and upset by the whole event. Our best friends have just left our home and we may have lost them for good. She doesn't blame me alone for the argument, nor even for the emotional heat we generated; in her view, we were all responsible for what we did. But my losing control again—so rare these days—was my responsibility alone. That, together with the strong possibility of our losing two good friends, to say nothing of ruining the end of an otherwise wonderful day, really hurt and disappointed her. I feel like I've failed again; I've hurt Anne, and I've behaved like an asshole!

Step 2. Recall the mental images that surfaced during this episode, but that might have come from previous experiences of perceived assaults upon your self.

Pictures of people with power and control in big church, big army, and big government were the mental images that came up for me in this episode. But then, they always did. The words used, the facts imposed, the authoritative tones of voice all reminded me of that superior knowledge and power claimed—in my experience—by the religious, military, and political elite. Corresponding images were of me and my kind as the underdogs, fighting for recognition, respect, and equality.

Step 3. Recall the emotional feelings you had during this episode that seemed more intense than the event itself and might relate to those previous experiences.

Humiliation, rejection, put-down, resentment, guilt, shame, personal attack, crushing defeat, worthlessness, and ignorance. These all seem to get mixed up with each other when I am angry, but they were the main feelings I could identify then. Looking back later, it all boiled down to pain and fear.

Step 4. Recall where, when, and with whom you have had those mental images or emotional feelings before this episode. Is there any sense of déjà vu?

My argument with Patrick was just that—a heated political argument. But my feelings of being put down, crushed, and defeated were fuelled by emotional baggage from my past.

(In a sense, this episode was a bit like the first of a series of windows that, when opened, showed me the pathway back through my emotional biography. Let me show you what I mean. By my opening the three biggest "windows" in my biography, you will see how I used them to go back and source the pain and fear that drove my anger. Notice how I start with the more recent events and work my way backwards.)

1. For six years I was a Member of Parliament in Western Australia, four as a government member and two as an independent. In that period, a whole series of irregular and confidential financial deals between government and business figures had been struck. I opposed all those deals on principle, but one in particular I campaigned against publicly.

   I was told (privately) that the deal would proceed regardless, that I was just an idealist and I shouldn't be getting involved in things that didn't concern me. Worse, I was labeled a traitor to the government.

   I felt the party, its members, our supporters, and the public as a whole were being compromised and betrayed by all those deals—but especially by this one. It seemed to me that all the values I cherished and believed in were being systematically destroyed. I felt crushed, failed, and defeated—just like when I was a kid.

   The night I lost it with Patrick, all those figures and faces, the people and events, the memories of unsuccessful confrontations and party-room debates had reemerged for me. I had recast my friends into old images of manipulative and self-serving bullies. But the emotional ways in which I had experienced the two quite different events, separated by a whole continent and six years, went back much further in my life.

2. As it was for many Vietnam veterans, the war in Vietnam was also a war within myself. I had volunteered to go at age nineteen, as a medical NCO with an infantry unit, the Fifth Battalion, Royal Australian Regiment.

My country (or at least its government) convinced me it was right to go, because according to the so-called Domino Theory, we were in serious trouble. If we didn't stop the communists in Southeast Asia, Malaysia and Indonesia were next—and then Australia.

My church (or at least its Catholic hierarchy) blessed our involvement (in the early years) because it was a "war against communism and the enemies of God."

On our return to the country that sent us away, we stood accused as child killers and brutes. We discovered we'd been misled by propaganda about a national risk that never existed. And the church now seemed to condemn that which it had blessed.

All that violence, bloodshed, friends lost or maimed, the nightmares, the wasted lives—all for nothing. The superior, the knowledgeable, and the powerful had had their way at our expense. These were the interests that Patrick and Simon seemed to represent and stand for on our front deck that night. These were the demons their arguments touched in me. Many of them had plagued me since I was a kid.

3. Throughout my childhood, the Catholic church played an all-consuming part in the life of our family. The faces and figures of priests and nuns and well-to-do people, superior authorities with knowledge and power, were always there to admonish us sinners. Ours was not to question but to accept their doctrine and dogma. They were the wise and selected, we the poor and grateful. Our welfare depended upon how much we toed their line, our salvation upon how much "God" might forgive.

Yet the same priests and nuns were there to encourage the potential saints in us. It was all about surrendering our selfhoods to God through the institution and authorities of the church. So again the superior, the knowledgeable, and the powerful held the keys to the kingdom and, therefore, to success.

That night on our deck, Patrick and his friend Simon had joined the forces of evil. Or, to put it correctly, I had recast Patrick and his friend into the images that haunted so much of my life. They had become the superior, the knowledgeable, the powerful. I, the rebel, had declared war against them. And, I had dumped on Patrick much more than his fair share of my anger.

Step 5. Recall previously forgotten painful or fearful events or periods from anywhere in your life that were resurrected by this anger episode or by the review you are doing right now.

At one point in our argument, the issue of law-breaking came up. Patrick hurled at me that violent people should be lined up and shot like dogs—that way they couldn't do any more harm. That evoked new and different recollections of the Vietnam War for me. All of a sudden, my part in that violent war came back to haunt me. Looking back at that single year, now three decades ago, I found myself suddenly aware of a time in my life when I did, in a sense, live violently and in fear of violence.

I thought I had resolved all that Vietnam War stuff years ago. I have never quite resolved the Catholic stuff, nor my rebellion against authority in all its forms.

Step 6. Review steps 2–5 of your BioScan, and identify those mental images, emotional feelings, déjà vu events, and previously forgotten painful or fearful events that you sense might have been driving your anger during the episode recalled in step 1.

From step 2: Patrick and Simon reminded me of all those people in my past in positions of authority and superiority. Their perceived superior knowledge and imposition of it always made me feel inferior, ignorant, and stupid. I used to burn with anger inside at that, but I could never say so in my early life for fear of retribution and humiliation. As a child, I was always punished in some way for daring to question superior authority—especially in primary school, boarding school, and church.

From step 3: My recurring feelings were humiliation and resentment at the fact that it always seemed to be me who was wrong and they who were so bloody right. Since I was taught throughout my Catholic childhood that my selfhood didn't count in the scheme of things, I grew up believing I had no right to succeed at anything for myself—only for God. It wasn't too different with politics.

From step 4: My experiences in politics, at university, and in some of my community and professional activities were bitter fights hard won, often at some personal cost. So, it felt as if Patrick and Simon were challenging and ridiculing the value and validity of those personal, professional, and political fights.

From step 5: Fear of violence emerged as a long-forgotten but unresolved issue for me. Although I was seriously angry at Patrick and Simon, I knew I was risking a physically violent confrontation, yet I pushed them to the limit. I guess it was my fear of physical violence, rather than my commitment to nonviolence, that drove me to throw my glass at the driveway instead of throwing a punch at Patrick.

Step 7. Identify those issues of pain and fear you need to own and deal with to defuel your anger.

I need to deal with my resentment of authority. I don't need to stop being critical or questioning, and I don't need to start fearfully giving in to authority again. I have experienced so much pain and cost whenever I have given in without questioning the implications. But I do need to get some balance, and to recognize that there are other legitimate points of view to be offered and decisions to be made that I won't always like or be comfortable with. And, I need to see that those points of view or decisions are not always a personal attack or an assault upon my self.

I need to work at not seeing or framing people through my emotional lenses of superiority versus inferiority. I need to throw away those lenses and substitute them with a pair that doesn't cause me quite so much pain.

My fear of ignorance—of not knowing something, of not having the answer—sometimes gets in the way of my otherwise good listening skills. So I don't listen to what's really being said, only to my fear of what might be implied by my interpretation of what's being said. It's as if my anger comes up to protect me from what I fear I might resent or reject. And then I'm in trouble.

I set myself up in a double bind; I don't want violence, exposure (as ignorant or stupid), or personal loss (of face, of confidence, of "knowing"). To protect myself from exposure and loss, I get angry, and if it's serious enough, I expose myself to violence instead. It's as though I'm still at war somehow. So I need to work on three more issues:

- My fear of violence (not the same as my opposition to it)

- My fear of exposure (writing my own BioScan is helping with that)

- My fear of losing (I thought I had resolved this in politics— maybe I never did).

benjamin's bioscan

Benjamin (not his real name) did his BioScan on his own as a take-home task associated with his counseling. I gave Benjamin the form you have already looked at on pages 79–84.

I also gave him my own BioScan to use as an example—just as you are invited to use both his and mine now. Notice how he too tracks back through his "windows," from present events to past experience, to source the pain and fears that drive his anger.

With Benjamin's permission, I have reproduced his Bio-Scan almost exactly as he wrote it.

Step 1. Recall your last serious anger episode.

I was visiting a friend, talking about and searching for answers to my marriage breakdown. I was asked what effect the lack of children had had on our marriage. How had I coped with our attempts to have children? What did I think about the IVF [in vitro fertilization] program?

I explained that there was little or no counseling before or after the program (which took place many years ago). There was a "nice" nurse who gave me a jar to ejaculate semen into and a couple of "magazines" and sent me away to "perform."

As I was speaking with my friend, a feeling of desperation overcame me, a lump was filling my chest, and tears poured uncontrollably. I felt dizzy and closed my eyes. I was gasping for breath and feeling frightened. Each time I opened my eyes the room was spinning and flashing with light. I felt helpless. I couldn't suppress the anger and frustration I felt, bottled up for fifteen to twenty years.

Step 2. Recall the mental images that surfaced during this episode, but that might have come from previous experiences of perceived assaults upon your self.

While I was in school, my image of myself was that of a failure. A later image was of myself "not caring for my dying father." And another was of me never getting the proper reward or recognition for all the work I'd done.

I developed a "healthy" disrespect for teachers, air cadet sergeants, all those "do as I say, not as I do" people, bullying people who lead the way with threats—stated or implied.

Step 3. Recall the emotional feelings you had during this episode that seemed more intense than the event itself and might relate to those previous experiences.

I would describe my emotions as terror, frustration, humiliation, anger, fear, weakness, lack of self-control, fright, inability to argue without becoming angry, injustice, being outnumbered, failure, loss of face, can't win, loss of control, fear of being wrong, rejection, ignorance, hurt, inferiority, being overwhelmed, and guilt—all confused and bundled in together.

Step 4. Recall where, when, and with whom you have had those mental images or emotional feelings before this episode. Is there any sense of déjà vu?

I recall the day in grade six when we had to run across the school field. Those who could run fastest became eligible for official school sports day events or even for school teams that would compete against other schools. The rest of us were allowed to watch, but I was humiliated. (I remedied that later in life!) [Benjamin became an athletics coach.]

During my marital dispute I was involved in a motor accident. When the dust of the collision settled, I mouthed a couple of good four-letter words at the offender. But I was all charm and understanding when the other driver apologized and admitted fault. I cursed him later when I was going through months of discomfort and while my insurance company delayed payment. The case was so clear; why couldn't anybody see it my way? I was angry, frustrated, and hurt.

An evening with friends was spoiled when they began complaining about the number of holidays and amount of work teachers have to do. (My wife was a teacher.) I argued that they had a right to involve themselves in their children's education. But couldn't they see how lucky they were to have children to care about? My anger, frustration, and grief influenced my argument. I didn't see parenting as a right but as a pretty good way to live. I would have given my "testicles" to have children!

Step 5. Recall previously forgotten painful or fearful events or periods from anywhere in your life that were resurrected by this anger episode or by the review you are doing right now.

While I was running home from work one evening, a man made an insulting remark. Because I'd received several other insults earlier on the run, I told him to "get stuffed." I also suggested that when *he* could run, *then* he might have the right to criticize. Luckily he was a one-hit man; he hit me and almost knocked me off my feet. I felt vulnerable, naked, fearful, and weak. I also felt a great loss of face and an awful sense of injustice.

Step 6. Review steps 2–5 of your BioScan, and identify those mental images, emotional feelings, déjà vu events, and previously forgotten painful or fearful events that you sense might have been driving your anger in the episode recalled in step 1.

From step 2: Images of being a weakling, unworthy: "We are not worthy to gather up the crumbs under your table" (from *The Book of Common Prayer*).

From step 3: Constant childhood reminders of inferiority and all adults being "right." People in positions of authority seeming to abuse their positions and the power that goes with them.

From step 4: Humiliation—can't I do anything right? I try to lead a nonviolent life; I try to walk away. Nothing goes my way. Why am I a "garbage mouth"?

From step 5: Weakness, humiliation, fear, lack of confidence.

Step 7. Identify those issues of pain and fear you need to own and deal with to defuel your anger.

- I need to discover and understand myself.

- I need to assert myself.

- I need to challenge myself.

- I need to confront and deal with my problems.

- I need to take control of me.

- I must not constantly suppress my anger, but learn to express it in positive and healthy ways.

Benjamin's step 7 issues, although perhaps less clearly related to the earlier steps than the ones I discovered when doing my BioScan, provided the agenda for our remaining counseling sessions. He succeeded in healing much of his emotional pain and resolving his fears. He rarely gets angry these days.

Did you notice a common theme that stood out in both Ben's and in my BioScans? It's this: Most of us men who have a problem with anger—including myself—spend a lifetime blaming other people for making us angry. Yet via our BioScans, Benjamin and I found out it was our *own* emotional issues that made us angry, issues that contained both fear and pain, neither of which emotions could we "real men" allow into our masculine experience for fear of being somehow lesser men. All the men to date who have completed the BioScan have learned the same thing: that the source of their anger lay in their own emotional experience, and the only people who "made them angry" were themselves.

your bioscan

Okay! You've read the material involved in the BioScan several times now. You've worked through "Compiling Your BioScan." You've seen how I wrote my BioScan and how Benjamin wrote his. Now it's your turn.

getting started

You may be feeling a little daunted. Fine—but don't be deterred. Don't cancel on yourself. Just take some time out to think about—and *feel* about—what you have just read. And remember, this process is usually done in my consulting rooms, not between the pages of a book like this. So if you are having trouble with it, please be assured that you are quite normal. If it reassures you at all, remember that your BioScan is confidential. Benjamin's is under a fictitious name, but my own is published for all the world to see. I can tell you that exposing this personal information took some courage. Your BioScan will demand courage of you, too. I can only ask courage of you if I am prepared to set an example of courage myself.

This probably will be the first time in your life that you have stopped to review your anger in quite this way. So don't expect to grasp it all in one hit. However, to repeat one of my earlier cautions:

Do not think your way through your BioScan **intellectually,** no matter how much you might want to rationalize or explain your anger away. **Feel** your way through the task **emotionally,** no matter how hard, no matter how painful your anger is to you or those around you.

Feeling and experiencing, instead of thinking and rationalizing, might be new even for the most emotionally practiced of us men. I have been doing this work with people (including myself), on and off, for around twenty-five years. I wrote my latest BioScan specifically for this book—and it took me well over two hours of difficult self-searching and faithful recording.

Basically, in all the experiences you go through *internally* with your anger, you need to identify as many as possible of those *assaults upon your self* that evoked feelings of pain or fear. Most likely, such feelings are well hidden away, "safe" inside your emotional memory, where you hoped they could never betray you or your manhood. The problem is that they keep coming out in anger. That is why your latest serious anger episode is the best channel available to you for accessing those feelings *today.*

Think of your anger episodes as a series of bushfires. When you fight a bushfire, you don't point your hose at the flame or the smoke, the things that are seen to do the damage, that pose the risks and carry the fire forward. That would be so much wasted water and effort. Instead, you point your hose at the burning fuel, the seat of the fire, the source of the blaze. But what happens when conditions are really bad, when visibility is really poor due to all the smoke and heat and flying embers? You "read" the flames to see and access the seat of the fire, the burning fuel beneath.

Don't focus so much on the *external* harm or damage you might have done already in your anger. You cannot undo what you have already done. Forget all that *self-blame* stuff; it is time to take *self-responsibility*—not just for your behavior, but for the feelings that drive your behavior.

Finally, when you are ready, now or in the next few days (no more than a week from now), set aside a period of no less than two hours—preferably half a day—and conduct your own BioScan. Follow each of the seven steps carefully and thoroughly. Don't shortchange yourself; this exercise is too important to you and those close to you.

At the end of the process, you will have answered the question "'what makes you so angry?" At last, you will be able to identify those emotional issues that drive your anger. Then you will be in a much better place to learn how to do something about them—and to change your life.

Finally, remember that you do not have to do your BioScan alone—you can get professional help. In fact, if you are having trouble with it, I highly recommend that you *do* get help. Just make sure, when you ask a counselor or other skilled professional to help you, that he or she is willing to read this book and follow all the tasks—especially the ones in this chapter.

With or without help, when you are satisfied that you have completed your BioScan as well as you can, take a couple of days of well-earned rest before you tackle Chapter 6.

defuelling your anger

Who dares, wins.

— *Motto of the Special Air Services Regiment,*
Australian Army

If you've made it this far, you've dared your demons and completed your BioScan, a step that may have been quite challenging. But take heart, because you are over the hump. This chapter will probably be a little less difficult. And after this one, it's all downhill.

freedom from anger

The Road Less Traveled, by M. Scott Peck, is a gem for anyone, whether they have just completed the BioScan or not. *The Road Less Traveled* opens with this simple line: "Life is difficult." It continues,

> This is a great truth, one of the greatest truths. It is a great truth because, once we truly see this truth, we transcend it. Once we truly know that life is difficult—once we truly understand and accept it—then life is no longer difficult. Because once it is accepted, the fact that life is difficult no longer matters.[1]

"Where there's life, there's hope," we are fond of saying. But "where there's life, there are problems to solve" is just as true. No problems? No life! No life? No problems! Simple as that. I would add with some force that freedom—which we are so ready to fight for—gives us the responsibility to solve our own problems in ways that we see fit. Justice, on the other hand, provides the same right for everyone else around us. That is why freedom and justice go hand in glove with each other.

A little further down his road, Peck makes this stinging point: "In attempting to avoid the pain of responsibility, millions and even billions daily attempt to escape from freedom."

So what has all this—about life being difficult and freedom being one big problem-solving exercise—got to do with the question "what makes you so angry?" and the task of defuelling your anger?

When you completed your BioScan, especially step 7, you identified the emotional fuel that drives so much of your anger. Those step 7 issues are your problems to solve. If you are like most of us, you probably have spent much of your life *reliving your pain* and trying to *conceal your fears*—while they kept on coming up from underneath to fuel and heat your anger. Once you can resolve your pain and fears, you will break free of that cycle. But, consistent with life, the task is not easy—in fact, it can be quite difficult. Nonetheless, if you did the BioScan, you now have all the information you need to solve the problem of defuelling your anger. Believe me (and most of my clients): *That* is freedom!

The point M. Scott Peck is trying to make about freedom can be related to the problem of anger like this: If you want freedom from the intensity and frequency of your anger, with all of its risks of harm and damage, you have to own for yourself the issues that fuel your anger, as you identified them in BioScan step 7. Then you can exercise the freedom to resolve them so they do not fuel your anger quite so much anymore.

dealing with the issues

Resolving the issues is what we are going to try to do in this chapter. First, carefully read the Issues and Action Chart, below. Then see if you can identify any immediate distinction between those issues that relate to *past painful events* and those that relate to *present or future fears*. Don't commit yourself just yet, because some of your step 7 issues might not seem to fit instantly into one or the other group. There may be some overlap.

After you have familiarized yourself with the Issues and Action Chart, we'll discuss the matter of overlap between pain and fear. Then we'll discuss in more detail the task of assigning your step 7 issues.

Next, again using the Issues and Action Chart, we will take a look at some of the things you might have been doing with

issues and action chart

pain issues		fear issues	
Past Painful Events		Present and Future Fears	
What I have done or not done. What has been done or not done to me. What I have experienced, lost, or been denied that has cost or harmed me somehow in the past.		What I might do or not do. What may be done or not done to me. What I might experience, lose, or be denied that may cost or harm me somehow in the present or future.	
Pain Action Choices		Fear Action Choices	
I can:	I can:	I can try to:	I can:
Relive my pain	Relieve my pain	Conceal my fears	Confront my fears
by:	by:	by:	to:
Resisting it	Relenting	Fighting them	Resolve them
Repaying it	Relinquishing it	and/or	and/or
Repressing it	Releasing it	Fleeing them	Learn to live with them
Recycling it	Resolving it		

your emotional pain and what you could start doing differently to defuel your anger. These are what I call your "action choices." After that we'll do a similar, but slightly different, review of your action choices around your fears.

When you have completed the emotional work in this chapter, you should be equipped with the basic information you need to start owning and dealing with your pain and fear. You should discover a new freedom as you let go of those life-learned, unconscious tendencies to store them up as anger.

Make sure you have your step 7 issues on paper beside you while you work through the following sections. Relax, take your time, and go peacefully with yourself.

reviewing your issues

Although many will overlap, you should find that your step 7 issues can be classified into one or the other of two groups: those that cause you pain, and those that cause you fear. The issues you've identified will vary from reader to reader; I can only know the two groups into which, from my experience, they will fall. I call the two groups pain issues and fear issues. The Issues and Action Chart describes the two groups as we experience and respond to them now and offers choices for how we might respond differently.

Your first task is to review your step 7 issues and classify them under these headings by deciding whether each issue is more of a past pain or more of a present or future fear.

the overlap between pain and fear

There may be some overlap between pain and fear issues, as you discover that some of the painful events and experiences from your past are also at the heart of your fears now. They may have kept you from putting the issue to rest and getting on with your life. It might seem that you have been continuing to *relive* the issue because you have never been able to own and express the pain it caused you. In other words, you have never been able to *relieve* yourself of it.

For example, Benjamin, as he revealed in his BioScan, learned at school that he could not do anything right. His overriding image of himself at school was of a "failure," a "weakling," "unworthy." Some of the feeling experiences that went with those images included terror, loss of face, inability to win, fear of being wrong, guilt, and humiliation. Those experiences became reinforced by repetition in adulthood as his emotional memory or biography directed his fears, which in turn directed his action choices. Predictably, Benjamin's choices became self-fulfilling prophecies, setting him up to keep experiencing the same sorts of events, images, and feelings over and over again.

benjamin's story

Benjamin came into therapy after his marriage of thirty years had collapsed. Early in our first sessions, two outstanding features of his life and marriage emerged. One was that he had never asserted himself or his needs in any way for fear of rejection and humiliation—he was the "man" and (childless) "father figure" in their home. The other was that he and his wife had tried for the first fifteen years of their marriage to have children, about thirteen years of that on an IVF program. They failed; Benjamin was a failure again! "Bullshit!" you say. "Infertility is nobody's fault; it just happens." And you are right. But try telling that to a man who has always been labeled a failure.

So Benjamin's emotional biography of failure drove his fear of failure, which drove the choices he made to avoid or limit any actions or decisions on his part that might fail. So he never asserted his needs, and he never had them met—openly and directly.

How angry was Benjamin? Very angry... inside!

What did he do about it? After the couple's differences came to a head when Benjamin was in his fifties, he finally left home.

Now Benjamin wants to return and rebuild his life with his wife—his life partner, as he sees her. To do that, or to live a new life independently of her, Benjamin is learning new ways of dealing with old pain and fear. He has been relieving instead of reliving his pain, that is, learning to express it (relent), to let it go (release it), and to come to terms with it (resolve it). Now Benjamin's emotional biography doesn't run his life so much, because he is able to learn from it and use it. The big thing Benjamin learned was that he could find the courage to own and confront his fears and to take risks with them. Some he has resolved or is in the process of resolving. Others he is learning to live with—courageously.

Benjamin had the other, nonviolent, kind of problem with his anger: He suppressed it. He has not suppressed it since the episode he described in step 1 of his BioScan. You will be pleased to learn that in the time since I started writing this book, Benjamin has not only solved his anger problem, but has also reunited with his wife. And they're both happy!

assigning your issues

The choice between pain and fear may be arbitrary. But it doesn't really matter, as long as the category to which you assign your step 7 issues helps you to resolve them by changing your action choices, that is, what you will do about them from here on. And you may assign any one issue to both groups.

There are two simple questions you can ask yourself about each issue you identified that will help you decide where to assign it:

Question 1: What makes me _____? (do, feel, think, etc.)

or

Question 2: What stops me from _____? (doing, feeling, thinking, etc.)

Hint: I always use, and encourage my clients to use, action or doing words (verbs) in preference to naming words (nouns) when trying to describe an experience or a behavior.[2] Check the BioScan examples in Chapter 5 and you will see that both Benjamin and I have used verbs and verbal clauses to describe our step 7 issues.

Let's use two of Benjamin's step 7 issues, from pages 94–95, to apply the above two questions, as I would do in therapy.

Benjamin's first issue: "I need to discover and understand myself."

(Benjamin and I would also have a conversation about what specifically he needs to discover and/or understand about himself, but we'll overlook that here.)

Question 1: (Doesn't fit the issue, so let's try question 2.)

Question 2: "Benjamin, what stops you most from discovering and understanding yourself?"

Answer: "I'm scared to discover, and understanding myself means looking at things that hurt me."

Pain or Fear?: Write "need to discover" under fear; Write "need to understand" under pain.

Benjamin's final issue: "I must not constantly suppress my anger."

(Again, we would have a conversation about when, who with, and in what circumstances he suppresses himself generally and his anger specifically.)

Question 1: "Benjamin, what specifically makes you suppress your anger?"

Answer: "I'm scared to express it because I get into trouble if I do."

Pain or Fear?: Fear.

That is the basic strategy for assigning step 7 issues to pain or fear. Again, the assignment may be arbitrary, and you may want to assign an issue to both groups. On the other hand, you will find that some issues clearly fit into one group alone. If you are unsure, don't get hung up about it. Recognize that that particular issue probably fits for both your past pain and your present or future fear; assign it to both groups and just move on. It will make sense in the end.

Now that you have assigned your step 7 issues, we will consider some common ways in which we men relive our pain and conceal our fear in anger, and we will see how to deal with them differently.

issues for feeling and healing

"To heal it, you have to feel it," says Steve Biddulph in *Manhood.*[3] And how right he is. Yet how many of us spend most of our lives trying to avoid "feeling it"—unless the feeling falls into that group of so-called "positive" emotions?

And just what are the things we are supposed to feel and heal? Review again the step 7 issues you've identified and assigned to the category of pain, or to *both* pain and fear (that is, exclude those you've assigned only to fear). Notice that they all fit one or more of the descriptive statements listed in the top of the left-hand column of the Issues and Action Chart— things done or not done by you or to you; things you have experienced, lost, or been denied you in your life; things that have either cost you or harmed you somehow.

As you can probably guess, in trying to determine what your issues are for feeling and healing, you are not looking for the exhilaration you experienced when you graduated from high school or the great time you had on your wedding night— I'm sure you have no trouble retelling those stories over and over. You are looking for all those other events and experiences that have caused you deep emotional pain, but which you have put away somewhere and never dealt with.

It's important to rely for this information on your own accurate and complete record from step 7 of your BioScan. If I were to offer examples of what might constitute a significant event or experience that you need to feel and heal, I'd risk your discounting and discarding any of your experiences that don't seem to fit my examples. Therefore, I decided to forego giving examples here.

Your step 7 issues are valid precisely because *you* identified them via the process you went through in steps 1 to 6 of the BioScan. You will have to trust yourself enough to know that those really are the issues you need to work on. Be assured, if the issues you identified fit with the descriptive statements of the Issues and Action Chart, they are exactly the emotional events and/or feelings whose memories you need to heal.

When it comes to the painful events that have impacted most of us, some cruel paradoxes exist for many men:

- Instead of getting the *relief* we so badly need and to which we feel entitled, we seem destined to keep *reliving* these events, consciously or unconsciously, through our anger.

- As "real men" we learn we must *resist* our pain, instead of *relenting* and owning it.

- We might "act out" our pain on those around us, as though we could somehow *repay* or avenge the people or events that originally hurt us. We'll "get them back one day"; we never surrender or *relinquish* an opportunity to redress the cause of that pain.

- Our "manhood," our masculinity, demands that we control and *repress* our pain so we can get on with being a "man." And thus, it never quite gets let go of or *released*.

- Try as we might, our pain just keeps coming up for *recycling* in each angry outburst, never getting to be *resolved* once and for all.

These are the most common ways in which, unwittingly, unwillingly, and perhaps unconsciously, we relive our pain instead of relieving it. Feel the impact this truth has on your anger; sense the way your relived pain affects your emotional "bank balance" when you get angry. Then imagine how your life, your relationships, and your future emotional biography might look if only you could actually relieve your accumulated pain. Imagine how your next anger episode might proceed quite differently if it were defuelled of all that extra emotional baggage you carry around.

other men's stories of feeling and healing

The first story comes from Steve Biddulph's *Manhood*, in which he tells of his friend's awakening from anger to peace.

A friend of mine lost his father at the age of eight. His mother suicided two years later. He and his younger brothers were split up and sent to various relatives and rarely saw each other until adulthood. When I met him, he was a highly successful businessman, but troubled by sudden rages that had lost him a number of employees. He had two failed marriages and was just holding on in a third. By now he knew that the problem was in him, and was ready to talk. All he really needed to do was tell the story [relent] and express the grief [release] that went with it. A simple, profound act which he had never done, with anyone, since childhood. As he told his story, softly and slowly, he would suddenly be overcome with great washes of tears and sobbing. Then he would quietly go on. Gradually the most extraordinary feeling of peace came into the room where we were sitting. It's an experience I will never forget.[4] [Additions in brackets are mine.]

That simple story is also the story of a hundred different men I've seen in my rooms. I love Steve's telling of it, so simple and graphic, with such humility.

chas's letter

The second story comes from a letter from one of my clients after he completed therapy. Chas was a thirty-year-old salesman who, when he first came to me, had left work voluntarily after engaging in several serious (but not physically violent) episodes of anger towards his boss and colleagues. He had also been physically abusing his wife; as a condition of my agreeing to see him, he had taken up residence away from home to protect his wife's safety and the emotional welfare of their child. He had also assaulted one or two other men unrelated to his family or work. Chas was becoming more intensely and frequently angry, easily given to losing control and reacting violently to any stress.

From a childhood and adolescence where violence in one form or another was common, and where expectations to perform were enforced punitively and unrealistically, Chas grew up with his emotions well shut down—except for his anger. That only began to show outwardly in his late twenties. His golden rule for survival was more than just "don't *show* your feelings"; it was "don't *have* any feelings." To do otherwise as a kid was to be punished; as an adult, having feelings had become impossible. Hence no one, other than his wife, had ever invited Chas to discover, own, or express his feelings. The only way he knew how (until now) was in anger and violence.

I thought you might appreciate his letter:

Dear Frank,

I'd like to thank you from the bottom of my *heart*. Knowing now that's where it all comes from and not my past thoughts. Being able to *think with my heart* has made me *feel new* and has given me another chance with my family and my life. You've also given me the initiative to think what I want instead of living up to everyone else's expectations. I know I still have a fair way to go but *I feel it getting easier every day.* That initial thought when you think it's all falling apart is so vital and it's easy to step on the wrong side (love/hate). *It's so much easier to wear your heart in your mouth rather than sticking your fist in someone else's.* [emphasis mine]

Thanks. Chas.

Chas and his wife still have their problems, but they have been back together for over four years. She feels safer with him. He is also back at work and doing well. His anger is much less intense and less frequent, and he has not done anything physically violent for five years.

what changed for these men?

Like Biddulph's friend, Chas no longer feels obliged to resist, repay, repress, or recycle old, unexpressed pain. On the contrary, he is at last free to express and release it. Notice how Chas describes his experience as "feeling new." Additionally, Chas also uses some practical strategies of the kind you will find in Chapter 8.

It is very humbling to work with someone like Chas; I shall treasure his letter always. More importantly, Biddulph's story and Chas's letter let you see how an angry life can be transformed—how when you own and open your emotional channels, you can start to express and release all of yourself, instead of keeping half of yourself imprisoned under lock and key. So let's start opening ourselves to some new action choices for dealing with emotional pain.

pain issues: your action choices

Using the Issues and Action Chart, let's go through some of the things you might have been doing with your pain up to now, and some of the new things you could start doing from here on.

resisting versus relenting

Resisting emotional pain is like denying that it hurts.

Recall the last time you were doing a really heavy job. Maybe you were trying to lift something too heavy, trying to increase the amount you lift at the gym, moving some really heavy piece of equipment at work, or digging a trench through clay and rock. You were determined to succeed, but it started to really hurt your back, your arms, your shoulders. Still, you kept going (men do that, don't they?), and to get through the job, you just kept convincing yourself that the pain was nothing or even that it didn't hurt at all. Nothing was going to stop you, so until you reached your goal, you resisted the pain on the basis that "it's all in the mind."

There are only two possible outcomes here. Either the pain stops when you finish the task (although you might experience some tired and aching muscles and joints later), or you injure yourself. Either way you grin and bear it; later, if the injury gets in your way or disables you, you might **relent** and go to the doctor. Finally, you are forced to agree that it did hurt after all—the evidence is in the injury, obvious and inescapable. But it's all a bit too late. If only you had relented earlier and "listened" to the pain as a signal that you really needed to be going about that job differently! But next time, you do it just the same way—and the next time, and the next time, and the next time after that. Oh how stubborn we men can be!

It's a lot like that with emotional pain—only worse.

It can be okay for us men to learn from our experience of serious physical pain. We even have occupational health and safety rules in most workplaces that promote better and safer work practices. Modern men are starting to become more conscious about safety and are beginning to experiment with new ways of doing physical tasks. New technology has helped a lot, too.

But when it comes to emotional pain, we seem much less willing to learn the lessons. There's a whole manhood thing there, a complicated and intangible set of ingrained ideas about denial of or resistance to pain. It is considered "noble" and "manly" in our culture to resist emotional pain, wherever it comes from. And, it is regarded as "weak" and "unmanly" to relent and listen—to do things differently.

It can be liberating to relent to the pain.

perry's story

In dealing with his long-lost natural father, Perry was like the man doing the really heavy job. It wasn't a problem he couldn't deal with, he thought. Anyway, the pain he felt about being abandoned was nothing compared to what he had to put up with from his stepfather, his mother, and his first wife. Perry's pain about his lost father he could handle; it was "lightweight" and he'd "learned to live with it years ago."

Out of the blue, Perry's natural father phoned just before Christmas (he had found Perry's number through directory assistance). He announced that he was coming to Victoria between Christmas and New Years, and he "might be able to squeeze in a visit or a meeting," if Perry wanted that. Perry was excited, but apprehensive.

When his dad did come to Victoria, however, he did not see Perry. He phoned again briefly to say he just couldn't fit him in after all. No apology, no explanation, just couldn't make it. So the last time Perry saw his father remained the same: twenty-seven years earlier at age two!

Perry called me and sobbed his heart out over the phone. He had never allowed himself to acknowledge the pain or to grieve his loss until now. Perry is learning how to relent and own the pain of this loss that has had such profound impact upon his sense of self-worth and has made its own contribution to his anger. Ironically, instead of feeling less of a man, he now feels more complete as a man.

Maybe Perry's father did something useful after all. Hell of a way to do it, though!

can you relent and let go of your pain?

Review your pain issues. Can you relent without threatening your manhood? Can you purposefully revisit your most painful memories—the ones you identified through your last serious anger episode and your BioScan? Can you see how they might stop driving your anger once you stop resisting or denying the pain they hold for you?

Maybe you need to sound off or rage at the event. Or, maybe you just need to grieve a little, cry a little, by yourself or with someone you feel safe doing that with.

The action choice is yours to make. You can just button up or batten down and tough out the pain until the next time you injure yourself or someone else in anger—or you can open up, let the barrier down, and own the pain as yours so you become free to go about the task of dealing with it differently. You can keep up the resistance, or you can relent; the choice is yours.

repaying versus relinquishing

This is a difficult choice for most men because it touches our sense of fair play and justice. Enormous courage is needed to move from a commitment to *repay* an injury, a wrong, an injustice, or any assault upon the self to a decision to let it go and get on with life. The problem is we rarely if ever actually get to repay our wrongdoers, especially if the event was somewhere in our past. But even recent wrongs are often hard or even impossible to right when the damage has been done or when we lack the resources, skills, opportunity, or power to do so. Instead, we just carry them around like so many monkeys on our backs, saving them up to "get even."

But guess who cops our accumulated wrath over all those wrongs? Every time we get angry at some event or person who just happens to pull the trigger, out it all comes, full bore, both

barrels—in loads more than the "trigger-puller" actually de-
serves, just like poor Patrick, who copped it all from me. (See
my BioScan in Chapter 5.) The worst part is that in the end we
cop it *ourselves* every time we weigh ourselves down with the
guilt-ridden hangover of each anger episode.

There is a cruel irony at work here. A much-cherished feature of manhood in our culture is a man's courageous willingness to "fight" for freedom if ever it is seriously threatened. In
the Australian culture in which I live, Australian men are seen
as having a history of fighting wars for the freedom and
defense of others, and a record of opposing any imposition of
authority at home that might curtail our own freedom. American men are seen as having a similar history by those who
share their culture. Yet, when it comes to freeing ourselves
from the emotionally tyrannical dictates of masculine culture,
we often "wimp out." Letting go of a wrong is regarded as cowardly surrender rather than courageous liberation.

damon's story

Damon worked for a company that had responsibility for cleaning public toilet facilities in several local government areas.
One day Damon saw a small piece of trash lodged between a
cistern outlet and the wall behind it. He couldn't get it out
with his broom, so he groped with his hand to extract it. As his
hand closed on the trash, he felt something sharp pierce his
skin. The trash proved to be a hypodermic needle from a
syringe, probably dropped there by an intravenous drug user.

Damon feared he might have been contaminated with HIV.
He was medically examined and tested for the virus with negative results then and again three months later. He was also
advised that these negative results were based upon statistical
probability, *not* medical certainty. Damon became convinced he
was seriously at risk and that he might have as few as three or
as many as seven years to live. He was furious at the contract-
ing company for not taking protective action with the local

authorities, and with the local authorities for not securing its public toilet facilities against drug users.

Damon's anger took over his life from then until just recently, in his latest therapy sessions. He was driven by his commitment to "repay in full" the company for its negligence and the local authority for its failure. He rationalized that it was up to him alone to force both parties to take the corrective action he thought necessary, not just on his behalf but to protect the public as a whole.

Damon's principle probably was sound enough, and had he joined with his colleagues or approached his union or the relevant health authorities, he might have succeeded in effecting some contribution to the process of public health improvement. But Damon was too angry, too driven by his own personal pain at his threatened loss and potential harm. He would not relinquish either his pain or his crusade to anyone else.

Realistically, Damon was one man alone, a cleaner with no power, few negotiating skills, and no networking resources with whom he was willing to share. Nobody listened to his complaints; nobody had to, because Damon was in no position to cause significant difficulty to anybody but himself. It was tragic to witness his angry assaults upon himself as he failed and then blamed himself for failing, as he demanded redress and refused all opportunities to achieve it—unless he could do it alone.

While I was writing this chapter, I got a call from Damon. He was depressed but holding out his hand for help to move forward. "Yes, I will go to my union and the health authorities for help—later!" First he wants to heal. He is now ready to *relinquish* the battle and get on with his life.

dare to relinquish your fight . . . and win!

What about you? Are you ready to relinquish your crusade against whatever unrightable wrongs you might have stored in your emotional biography?

Check your whole BioScan again, not just your step 7 issues, to see if there are any unwinnable campaigns in which you are enmeshed or committed. Consider how many of your anger episodes those campaigns have infiltrated.

- Whom or what were your shots really aimed at, and who did they *actually* hit?

- Whom or what were you trying to repay, and who *actually* paid the price?

- For how long, and how many more times, will you load your anger with the wrongs of the past in how many doomed to fail bids to repay them?

Ask yourself, "Wouldn't I rather relinquish, so I can heal and get on with my life?"

repressing versus releasing

Repressing emotional pain is similar to resisting but goes further and deeper. This is not so much about knowing "it" hurts, but more about pressing ahead in good old manly fashion until you injure yourself or someone else. This is more about not even knowing "it" is there to hurt you until you bring "it" up to consciousness and take a look.

(Unfortunately, the idea of repression may conjure up the controversial issue of so-called "repressed-memory syndrome," a debate that currently rages around the question over the validity of repressed memories of childhood sexual abuse. Whatever you feel or think about that issue, it is worth reviewing your BioScan to see if you get any sense of painful events that you may have buried deeply in your emotional unconscious memory.)

Let me quote a story of release from Steve Biddulph's *Manhood*:

A close friend of mine is a calm, urbane professional and a family man. He had a father who was quite the opposite—erratic and moody, given to outbursts of sudden violence. My friend recalls being about eight years old and his father asking him to come on a trip. The boy was scared. He hid behind his mother's skirts and did not want to go. While the father yelled and stormed about the house in a rage, the boy went to his bedroom and got into bed. Moments later the father burst into the room, lifted the whole bed and upturned it on top of the boy who was then held beneath it on the floor, screaming on the inside, on the outside silent with terror. It was good that the father didn't kill him, but bad that it happened at all. There were many similar incidents.

When the boy grew up, he became a career-driven achiever, yet never felt really happy. Only with the onset of midlife did the pain of these experiences begin to catch up with him—to pour out of his body. He began experiencing all kinds of alarming physical reactions—panic attacks, sensory distortions—but luckily did not panic or run for tranquilizers. Through talking over the experiences, he made the link with his childhood and accessed many memories that had not so much been forgotten as pushed down as too painful. In time, and with help, he became more at ease with himself, able to take better care of himself and emotionally more peaceful and flowing. He also made major career changes, took long holidays with his family, and set about a very different rhythm of life based on fulfillment, rather than external achievement.[5]

This story is not, so far as we can tell, one of anger and rage, although it could just as easily have been. Certainly in my own experience with men whose childhoods were marked by similar traumas and in whose early adulthood the pain was well repressed, anger and rage have been common vehicles through which "to pour out of [their bodies]" all that pain.

Notice the major changes Biddulph's friend was able to make in his life once he was able to access the *repressed* pain of childhood trauma and to consciously *release* it from captivity.

Review your BioScan for sensory hints or overt messages about early life events whose associated pain you may have repressed. Now is the time for you to access and release that pain—and to change your life.

recycling versus resolving

This is the one we're all familiar with, where we keep opening and reopening old wounds over and over, never quite *resolving*, just *recycling* them. These are the painful issues we might run up the flagpole any time we get angry, and whoever is in the way better look out!

For me, it is either the church, Vietnam, or politics—sometimes all three. Thank God I am choosing to resolve them, one at a time, at last. They don't drive my anger or run my life nearly so much or so often these days. I am at peace, most of the time, with the much more humane face of a God who, with some help, I found inside myself recently. For years I haven't ducked for cover every time a truck backfires at night, and regardless of those terrible events in Vietnam and at home thirty years ago, I know I am not a child killer. As for my experience with politics—well, that is not buried yet, but it is certainly dying (in more ways than one!).

But you wouldn't have wanted to be around me all those years when I just kept bringing those events back and back and back to fuel and drive my anger. It was as if I were a furnace inside; I just kept opening up that furnace every time I got angry and saying to myself, "Gee! There's nowhere near enough heat in there." Then I would scurry around with fuel buckets and chuck in a corpse from Vietnam or some sanctimonious priest or a lying politician or two and give it a real good stoke-up. Twenty degrees higher instantly—it worked every time!

"EPRS" you could have called me: Emotional Pain Recycling Specialist!

michael's story

Michael had a similar but deeper problem. For him, it was the terrible pain of being sexually abused by three different "friends of the family" between the ages of ten and fourteen, made worse by his overwhelming sense of guilt for not being able to protect his sister from a similar fate at the hands of one of his older "friends." The fact that he was only eleven when his sister was raped and that he was unable to protect himself from his own abusers took a couple of very intensive therapy sessions to sink in. Michael's struggle for self-forgiveness was long, slow, and painful. Although he still has problems, Michael no longer sees those painful images every time his girlfriend asserts herself or someone has a go at him, so he hasn't been violently angry for some time. He has resolved most of the awful pain from those traumatic years of his childhood and doesn't recycle it so much these days.

Have another look over your pain issues to see what, if anything, you're still recycling through your angry episodes. You might need help to resolve these issues. If you do, find someone you can trust to just listen without judging you. It is important that this is a person who can honor your pain without harassing you to "just drop it."

The issues we recycle are among the hardest ones to deal with. Don't hesitate to find help if you feel you need it.

fear issues: your action choices

Let us review those step 7 issues you assigned either to the category of fear or to *both* pain and fear (that is, exclude those you assigned only to pain). Notice that these issues all fit one or more of the descriptive statements offered in the top box of the right-hand column in the Issues and Action Chart—

things you might do or not do or have done to you; things you might experience, lose, or be denied in your life; things that may *cost you* or *harm you* somehow.

We can try to *conceal* our fears. There is a lot in our culture of manhood that exhorts us to do just that. The problem is that we never really succeed in our attempts. Even trying to avoid them by skirting around the people and events that might expose us is an enterprise that depends more upon chance than it does upon our skill or our limited ability to control such people or events. What we are really doing with that life-limiting strategy is not so much hiding our fears as we are hiding *ourselves* from our fears. As the saying goes, you can run but you can't hide forever.

Some of the stories told by Vietnam War veterans about fear and courage—if you can ever persuade them to tell you much at all—often seem a little out of place, sort of trivial in the context of a war in which much bigger, more fearsome and dramatic events were happening daily. Here is one from my time in that troubled country.

frank's story: i confront my fear

The wet season in Vietnam is really wet—or it was thirty-odd years ago. The monsoon rains broke every afternoon around three o'clock. You could almost set your watch by it. During that season the rivers and creeks swelled and raced with unbelievable ferocity. To cross them during an operation, we'd sometimes be forced to make a handhold from bank to bank by tying our toggle ropes together. It was no joke to be the first or last man across—you'll understand why. Sometimes we'd just wade or half swim and half wade our way across in single file. You needed to be able to swim!

The army had an annual routine of TsOETs, or Tests of Elementary Training, which all personnel—especially in infantry units—were supposed to pass. As a medical NCO, I could always find ways of avoiding TsOETs. I had to—at the time I couldn't swim! My avoidance strategy worked well until Vietnam . . . and the wet season!

There's a certain river near Nui Dat in Phuoc Tuy province, South Vietnam; it's called the Sui Da Bang. It should have been called the Sui Da *Big*; in the wet season it was big and fast and very deep, or so it seemed to me. One day we had to cross the Sui Da Bang. Inexorably, I crept closer to the bank, separated from exposure or disaster by a single file of men getting shorter and shorter until it was gone. Then there was me. Yep! Just me, the Sui Da Bang, and my fear. The choice was straightforward enough—I either declared or drowned! Nowhere to run, no one to fight, nothing to hide behind or save me. But I'm still here to write about it, so I guess you know what choice I made.

I remember being angry at the river, the country, my company commander, the army, and the war. Sometime later it dawned on me that most of all I was angry at me—for all those stupid choices I had made to avoid opportunities to learn to swim, for evading TsOETs, for not owning up before we ever went to Vietnam. And, hey! What about all those lives I put at risk . . . and I was supposed to be the company medic!

Well, that was war back then, and this is peace right now. Or is it?

How much personal and interpersonal "war" could we avoid by making choices based on honest and open information about ourselves, our needs, and our skills and abilities or lack of them? If we could just learn to accept responsibility for those choices that we make every day of our lives, instead of blaming someone or something else, how angry would we get when we were confronted with our fears?

Look at my step 7 issues in Chapter 5. Who gains and who loses from my either *fighting* or *fleeing* my fear of not knowing something? Me, of course! That is what makes me angry at me, even though I might take my ignorance out on someone else by getting angry at him or her. And how "manly" is it to fight or flee my fear of violence? Doesn't it take more courage to own that fear, to *confront* it so I find the strength and courage to deal with my fear calmly, instead of provoking violence by my anger? And if I cannot *resolve* my fear, I still need to own and confront it so I can *learn to live with it*, courageously.

rajid confronts his fear

Remember Rajid from Chapter 3? His rule for survival, you'll recall, was "Don't get scared; get control." Rajid spent his life fighting his fear until he was led to confront it in therapy. Now he understands that he doesn't have to live with it so much any more. Rajid has resolved his fear of not being in control (over others) by separating his previously repressed childhood nightmare (real enough at the time) from his conscious adult reality. He knows about his fear; he also knows he has the skills and experience to deal with threatening situations by making different and better-informed choices about how to live his life.

now, what about you?

Are you ready to confront your fears? What scares you? What secret fears drive your anger?

Closely scrutinize the fear issues from your BioScan, and see if you can spot how your *fight* or *flight* responses to fear come out in your anger.

Can you resolve your fears, or learn to live with them, so they no longer secretly drive your anger?

What do you need to choose to do in order to confront your fears so you can either resolve them or learn to live with them?

One of the best ways, and the bravest, to own and confront your deepest and most secret fears is to find another man you know and trust and ask him to just quietly and patiently listen while you talk. If you can do this, you will be stunned by the way those newly expressed fears, communicated simply to another man, lose their power and control over you. Almost as certainly, you will notice that the man with whom you share your fears will start to look at you with something like admiration in his eyes for what he will regard as a display of uncommon courage. When you are finished, in all likelihood your listener will want to declare to you some fears of his own!

Best of all, you two will know each other and yourselves differently.

Try it. What have you got to lose but your fear...and some of your anger, of course!

defuelling your anger

Now that you're finished with the challenging work of this chapter, stop for a while and think about what it has always meant to be a man in our culture. (Yes, you can go back to "think" mode for a spell, where we men are more comfortable.) Ask yourself, "Do I really expect it to be easy to start burrowing around deep inside a lifetime of emotional pain and fear?" We men spend most of our lives rising above all that, not letting our feelings get in the way of the important things we are expected to do at work, at home, in sports, and elsewhere. For many of us, however, those awkward, secret, and "unmanly" feelings smolder away somewhere down there, like so much unspent fuel. The only time they are allowed to surface is when some person or event acts to throw another log on the fire, so it all flares up at once—in anger.

You identified that emotional fuel in Chapter 5 through the BioScan. In this chapter we have tried to develop a general emotional strategy for defuelling your anger. Make the strategy work for you in your next anger episode, and you won't cause the same risk of harm or damage. There won't be that same arsenal of unspent emotional fuel, to be stoked up again next time.

If your strategy doesn't work immediately, or not quite as well as you'd hoped, keep trying—it takes determination to succeed. Simply do your BioScan again, using your next serious anger episode as the channel to work through. Next, review the action choices you've been making against those outlined in the Issues and Action Chart. Then ask yourself again: "Have I been *reliving* instead of *relieving* my pain? Have I been *concealing* or *confronting* my fears?"

At the very least, you will feel better and more complete as a man, and you will notice your anger episodes decreasing both in frequency and intensity. And that is the primary goal of the BioScan process.

Either way, if you have come this far, you ought to congratulate yourself. This is challenging work for anyone to do. Please find some way of rewarding, or at least acknowledging, the courage and determination you've found to confront yourself emotionally the way you've been doing in these chapters.

the search goes on

Your search inside yourself goes on. You can use your BioScan over and over through the years, revising and adding to it as you go. If you still need outside help, *please* find a counselor or therapist who is skilled, experienced, and willing to work with your emotional biography.

Now, take a break for a couple of days; you've earned it. After that, we will get out of the navel and then head for the shed to discover some practical tools and strategies for *managing* anger effectively.

...then with your head...

preventing your anger

The greatest power we humans have is the power to choose; to do things differently.

— Anonymous

Welcome to the shed, the one place where we men can find real sanity in a psychotic world.

In North America, you call it the toolshed, or the shop, garage, or basement. In Australia, for as long as most men can remember—and most women who lose men to it—it's just "the shed."

The shed is more than just a structure. You can't buy what's in the shed (you can't sell most of it either, come to think of it). In fact, it's not a structure at all. The shed is a tradition. By whatever name you call it, and wherever you find men in families around the world, you'll find a version of the shed. Even if it's not really there, you'll find one somewhere in a man's heart. It's just, well, the way we men are.

The shed is a place where men do practical things, like fixing cars, repairing motors and electrical appliances, building cabinets and shelves, servicing bicycles and lawnmowers, mending broken toys and furniture, and so on. The shed is a place where a man uses his head and his hands, and loses himself from the world. Sometimes he loses his temper in the shed; other times he goes there to regain it. The shed is where a man keeps his best tools and equipment. It is full of mystery and mastery, and that is what has moved generations of kids to seek their fathers' company in the shed, or to steal secret glimpses when Dad is not there.

Where better than the shed—real if you have one, imagined if you don't—to devise some practical ways of preventing, releasing, and controlling your anger? In the shed we are going to check out some new and different tools and gauges and techniques for handling anger in very practical ways. We are going to learn ways to avoid the sorts of harm and damage that come from uncontrolled and serious angry episodes. We are going to reduce the risks we pose to people and relationships when we get angry.

We are going to be here in the shed for most of Part III. So pour yourself a hot cup of coffee and pull up a stool.

two ways to anger; one way to avoid it

There are two basic ways in which we set ourselves up to get angry, or experience ourselves as being set up (which is basically the same thing).[1]

First, there are the things we do ourselves. One of the more popular is to make sure we leave for work late so every other driver on the road is in our way and it seems to be out to get us. Another is to down a few beers, scotches, or glasses of wine to steel ourselves for an imminent marital argument, knowing damn well that alcohol controls anger the way a blowtorch controls a gas leak. Most of us men have our favorite ways of "liberating" anger. Do you know what yours are?

Second, there are the things others "do to us."[2] (They are never just "done"; they are always "done to us"; have you noticed?) The word *others*, of course, includes wives, children, employers, employees, colleagues, animals, vehicles (stationary or mobile), buildings, roads, weather (*especially* weather), rocks, trees, street signs, speedometers, clocks, and so on.

Because we seem unable to conceive of the possibility that it might actually be us—or, more specifically, what we do or don't do in response to their apparent provocation—we remain convinced of their criminal intent upon our selfhoods. After all, it is axiomatic that the more we boost our determination to be strong, resolute, and rational, the more the "enemy" targets our weaknesses, uncertainties, and emotions.

There is one way to avoid setting ourselves up for anger: **Begin to build a tool kit of different response capabilities to the same anger-arousing events.**

What do I mean? I will show you how I and a couple of my clients did exactly that.

the off button

A couple hours by road from Melbourne, the capital of Victoria, Australia, lies the pretty little country town of Daylesford. No wonder it is such a successful tourist attraction; as well as its location in the midst of a popular mineral-spa region, the town itself is peacefully caught in a time warp of old Victoria's rural heritage. Daylesford is pretty enough to visit, but its surrounding countryside is a magnificent example of healthy balance between quiet farmland and splendid forest. From 1995 to 1997, I was much more fortunate than the passing tourists; I got to commute through Daylesford, between Ballarat where I worked days and Woodend where I conducted a clinic two evenings each week. Mt. Macedon, the grand mountain on which I am privileged to live with my family, was ten minutes away from my last appointment.

Driving into Daylesford from Ballarat, you go through a "dead zone" where you can't get radio reception clearly—certainly not from FM stations anyway. The static crackles mercilessly, and the more you want to hear something, the louder it seems to crackle. So I start getting annoyed with it, and I can feel the anger rising up in me, and I start muttering things like,

"What's wrong with Daylesford; can't they fix this problem?"
"What's wrong with this radio station; how come they can't get a signal in here?"

Everything else—except me—is the problem or the cause of the problem. How dare they ruin my routine this way with nerve-splitting static that gets me so angry? Here we are in a new century, and you could swear Daylesford was locked into the last one!

The solution to this is the on/off button. So I push the off button, and guess what happens? It's fine. All of a sudden, instead of worrying about the awful radio reception, I am seeing the country and feeling it around me, even in my car. It is as if the bellowing cacophony that was invading my body through my ears is replaced by a quiet grandeur that penetrates my being through my eyes. I can sense the channel between me and nature, feel the peace that is there for the touching. And it is costing me nothing, not even a second of lost time.

That awful static is no longer bullying my receptors, rasping my nervous system, goading my anger. Instead...hey... this is nice country! Who needs Triple J? Who needs FM radio?

I guess the message is that sometimes **the best way to live in the world is to live *with* the world, instead of against it.**

So when you find yourself driving into "angry zones," it helps to have your own off button. Use the tools in the Anger Avoidance Toolkit, on page 139, to apply the off button in your daily routine.

the difference maker

David's favorite strategy for getting himself off to an angry start in the morning involved the family dog—his wife's dog, really. Tess had only had her new dog for about a year, and already it had taken up occupancy on the marital bed—always between David and Tess—much to David's irritation. Since

David was the first (human) up and about in the morning, and since he always brought coffee to Tess in bed before he had his own breakfast, confrontation with the "Hound from Hell" was inevitable.

Why? Because the first thing David saw when he went for the coffee was a soft brown turd right in the middle of the kitchen floor—every day!

As far as David was concerned, this dog was not his dog, he did not want it inside, and he definitely did not want it on or in his bed. He was getting sick and tired of getting up every morning to the mess in the kitchen. David was getting more than sick and tired; he was getting very, very angry.

Like Rajid in Chapter 3, David's life had been a series of war zones ever since his childhood skirmishes with his brothers, his own consequent abuse, and the ultimate barroom brawl with his father. If someone (human, animal, vegetable, or mineral) did something that David experienced as yet another assault upon his selfhood, then it must have been done to offend or threaten him in some way. So it followed that the "Hound from Hell" fouled the kitchen floor daily to offend and hurt him. Since the beast was owned by Tess, it also followed that it acted with her blessing. Evidence? Tess never did anything about it, would not allow the dog to be put out at night, and would never scold or discipline the beast. Therefore, the daily dog turd was a declaration of war from Tess.

Out came the guns.

First, the dog started getting kicked unceremoniously out the door, always *after* the event. Second, since David refused to clean up the mess, coffee and breakfast routines were disrupted and became very unpleasant, rushed affairs. Most early mornings ended abruptly with David slamming the door on his way to work (running late) after a bitter fight with Tess. Construction sites would be filled with tension as David, still angry, arrived to direct his crew. Hostilities between himself and his workers, contractors, and other associates were not uncommon. After a terrible day of tension, anger, and frustration,

David would become morose—even depressed—and guilt-ridden. He would make his unhappy way home to an unhappy wife and daughter, hoping to try to patch things up. The cycle grew worse over the weeks; things could not continue as they were. That was when David's physician referred him to me.

David and I did some pretty deep and painful emotional work together on the sources, experience, and damaging outcomes of his anger. Now we needed something practical. Somehow we came to see that the "Hound from Hell" offered an opportunity for David to try a practical experiment in changing one of the common ways he set himself up to get angry.

It was time to experiment, not with "guns" but with "roses."

The idea was David's. Not surprisingly, the best tools for change generally come out of your own toolshed. Here is an edited extract from one of our sessions:

Frank: It seems to me there are two things that piss you off about this issue; one's the dog, the other's the shit in the kitchen.

David: You're right!

Frank: You don't like the dog coming between you and Tess one little bit, but you hate with a passion what his mess does to your breakfast, your coffee routine, your fights with Tess, and the rest of your entire day. I mean, this is a case, David, where we could say literally that the shit has hit the fan—or was it the floor?

Both: Ha ha ha ha!

Frank: Seriously, David, it's taken over your whole bloody day—every day! Your life's being run by dog shit.

David: Now come on, Frank, surely it's not quite that bad. I mean, I could always clean up the bloody mess if it comes to that.

Frank: So what stops you?

David: What do mean what stops me? What kind of silly question is that? The bloody dog shits all over my kitchen. I can't make coffee for Tess in that, can I? And anyway it's her fault as much as the dog's—more! And how am I supposed to have breakfast and get myself off to work? I mean, you've got to be there, Frank; it's not just now and then, it's every bloody day, for God's sake!

Frank: So what stops you—from cleaning it up, I mean?

David: Frank, you don't understand. The dog shouldn't be doing it inside.

Frank: But it *is* doing it inside! And I'm just wondering, I mean, I know there are a lot of issues here about toilet training, hygiene, whose responsibility, and all that, but I was just wondering....

David: Wondering what? What were you wondering, Frank?

Frank: I was just wondering how things might be different for you—for you and Tess in the mornings, and for the rest of your day—if you did just clean up the mess. I mean, rub the dog's nose in it or whatever you're supposed to do, and then, well, just clean it up. I dunno, what do you reckon?

David: What do you mean? The bloody dog—Tess's dog—shits in the kitchen, and I'm supposed to clean it up?

Frank: No, no, no. I'm not saying you *have* to clean it up; I was just wondering how different things might be for you if you *did*. I'm just picking up on your idea; you know, you said, "I could always clean it up, if it comes to that."

David: Yes, well, I mean, I could, I guess. God, when I think of how much time, energy, and awful feeling go into those daily fights—the road rage on my way to work, the arguments at work, the accusations when I get home again—all that would be different, that's for sure. It would only take a couple of seconds to clean it up. Or, maybe I could offer to take the dog outside the night before; maybe we both could. Yeah, you might have a point.

But Jesus, Frank, I shouldn't have to, really.

Frank: Perhaps an experiment?

David: How do you mean?

Frank: You know, you agree to clean up the dog's shit every day for one week only. Every night you fill in the anger monitor we set up. Next session, we'll look at the results in terms of the frequency and intensity of your anger. We'll also look at the differences in your early morning routines and the rest of your working day.

If there's no change, or if things are worse, we abandon the experiment and go back to the status quo. Ditch the "roses" and return to the "guns."

David: Okay, I think you're on! One week it is; for one week only I clean up the dog shit. And then we'll see . . . .

David returned for his next appointment one week later. That some major and positive change had occurred was obvious when he came through my door. He was beaming, looked quite relaxed, laughed as he sat down, and proclaimed, "You're a dickhead, Frank Donovan, and I love you."

Bemused by his backhanded compliment, I asked him to explain.

"Well," he laughed, "We spent an hour and a half, the first time I came, discovering how fucked up and traumatized I must have been by my childhood. The second time we spent the last half hour talking nothing but dog shit—and you had the nerve to suggest that if I cleaned it up, things might be different. Only a complete dickhead would suggest such a thing— that a man's life could be turned around by picking up a dog's turd and flushing it down the toilet!"

"So how come you love me?" I asked shakily, contemplating the prospects of my whole professional credibility chasing that dog's mess down David's toilet.

"_Because it worked!_" he yelled.

"Don't get me wrong," he quickly added, "I hated cleaning up that bloody mess every day. _But_, Tess and I have not had one fight, I felt good getting her coffee again, I've enjoyed my breakfast every day this week, I yelled at nobody on the road, and the guys at work think I'm on Prozac or something. I've had a great week and I love you for that!"

I sat there stunned, excited—no, exhilarated—for him. All I could do was to touch his hand and say, "Great!" I was kind of speechless and humbled at the same time. Oh, I wasn't surprised the "experiment" had worked; as I said, the best tools for change come out of your own shed. It was David's excitement that really amazed me. For the first time in his life, he had been able to do something so different, so out of character—yet so simple (or was it?). The doing of it had actually undone his usual, familiar, internal experience of intensely disabling anger. More accurately, David now had emotional options available to him that he had never had before.

There was still a heap of emotional-growth work for David and me to do together over the remainder of our six-session program, but there was now a huge difference in his approach to our task. His enthusiasm and motivation had gone through the roof since he had experienced firsthand—at such a practical level—that he could actually change his emotional experience of anger before it reached threshold levels. By choosing to _do something different_ (clean up) _about the same event_ (the dog's mess), David had transformed the way he experienced the start of his day.

By so doing, he had also transformed the ways in which he was likely to experience the rest of his day and his relationships with other people.

At the age of fifty-two, and in construction work all his life, David was the kind who would insist, "I am what I am, and I'm too old to change." Yet now he was doing just that—changing! Understanding now how he sets himself up for anger, David remains able to choose to stop doing it.

David still gets angry—that's human—but it doesn't get in his way so much anymore. His relationships with himself, his wife, and others have improved out of sight.

David's got "the difference maker" now, and he knows how and when to use it.

His next challenge is to get the dog out of the marital bed. Last I heard, he was making some kind of deal with Tess about that; I don't know what it is, but David seems to smile a lot these days.

And that's a hell of a difference.

the risk taker

Jensen was twenty-seven years old and just two months away from his first wedding anniversary when he came to see me.

His American wife, Marion, had left him while he was at work one day and returned to the safety of her family in the United States. She had written to Jensen en route, explaining that she was unable to live with his volatile anger any longer. Marion felt controlled by fear and denied the right to express her own selfhood for fear that would provoke his anger.

For his part, Jensen felt Marion was experienced, worldly, competent, flexible; the decisive one of the two. Jensen didn't make decisions or choices about anything except his work, because he had learned from childhood that he was always inadequate, wrong, and incompetent. Jensen placed Marion on a pedestal, from which she both dazzled and embarrassed him.

In Marion, Jensen had come to see a mirror that reflected his own sense of inadequacy, inferiority, and incompetence. Although he loved Marion with his life, Jensen hated his reflection in her mirror, and therefore attacked and blamed Marion for "making him feel so stupid." Easily aroused to anger, he would yell and scream at her at home, or become enraged with jealousy and embarrassment at parties and other social events.

Operating from the emotional experience of fear, Jensen ironically was responding to that experience with blame and control. The more he blamed and attempted to control Marion, the more frustrated and unsuccessful he became, thereby reinforcing his sense of inadequacy, inferiority, and incompetence. As this vicious cycle intensified, Marion's fears for her safety and selfhood grew until she felt compelled to leave. So she did—and Jensen's world fell apart.

You will recall from Chapter 1 that my first priority here normally would have been for Marion's safety. Here was a classic case of a young man living an insoluble tension between his total dependency and need to be taken care of on the one hand, and on the other his burning need to control Marion and treat her as a prized possession, a trophy. His anger had reached a violent stage where harm was imminent. At this point, then, I would have asked Jensen to leave their home for a while to guarantee Marion's safety while he worked on his anger and attitudes. She, however, had acted on her own initiative to secure her safety and had returned to the United States.

My assessment was that Jensen's anger was not the first or even the most important problem to be addressed. What seemed much more immediate was Jensen's rigidly restricted response capability to his experience of fear (of being shown to be inadequate, inferior, and incompetent). Except for tasks at work, Jensen had almost no *conscious* experience of making significant choices or decisions about his own life or what he should and could do with it. He had lots of experience *blaming* others for his apparent inability to control his own life. In his blaming and fearful anger he unconsciously tried to control the lives of others.

Because of this, both our therapeutic work together and the tasks for Jensen that arose from our sessions were aimed at enhancing his experience and skills for making personal choices and decisions about his own life. Among other things,

Jensen had to find and use the *courage to fear* further exposure.

Yes, you read correctly—like very many men, Jensen needed to discover the *courage to fear*. Most men learn through their socialization, first as boys and then as young men, that fear is taboo, off limits, unmanly. Fearlessness, we learn, is the true mark of a man.

In my seminars, I like to tell audiences the simple truth about medals and decorations awarded for bravery during the Vietnam War: Not one purple heart or military medal, no Cross of Gallantry or Victoria Cross was awarded for *fearlessness* under fire, but only for *courage* under fire. If those brave combatants had been without fear they would not have needed courage. It was never the incoming fire that made their actions brave, but their acting in the face of their fear of injury or death. It's only when you confront men with the immediate likelihood of their annihilation that they will finally allow in and own their fear. Here then is the difference between a responsible, brave action and an irresponsible, stupid one. The first takes account of all the factors—including the effect my fear might have on my judgement and on my prospects for success or failure *and* survival or death. The second takes no account of my fear and therefore increases the risk both of mission failure and personal death—and that may well put other lives at serious risk.

In ordinary peacetime life, most of us do not get confronted with that kind of threat: More often we get confronted with the threat of being exposed as something less than manly. The worst of all those threats is to be seen as fearful or scared. Therefore, we do just about anything to avoid that: We blame and accuse, we rage and we fight. We allow fear no entry point to our awareness—if we can help it. And so in our anger we do stupid, irresponsible, destructive, and harmful things to people and property. By contrast, having the courage to let in and own our fear is what enables us to take personal responsibility for our emotional lives and our actions.

Jensen had to learn how to do that in order that he could take life's risks—big and little—without blaming someone else for the outcomes of his ill-informed choices. But that was going to challenge him to step outside the simple "code of manhood" he understood and in which he had grown up. Jensen needed to discover the *courage to fear*, so that he could start behaving more bravely in his life.

And that meant taking some pretty big emotional risks as he experimented with a whole range of choices and decisions. There were big ones, like writing to Marion and owning his anger, recognizing her fear, and accepting that she might never want to reconcile. There were medium-sized ones, like canvassing options about where and how to live independently if reconciliation was not to be (such as rent an apartment, share housing, buy a home). And there were little ones, about clothes, sports, entertainment, cultural interests, and so on.

Our last session together was several years ago. Recent feedback is that Jensen and Marion have reconciled, that he continues to experiment with his own choices and decisions, and that she feels it is okay to be herself. She has her own professional career again, and he rarely has anger episodes of anything like the fearful intensity that once threatened her safety and their relationship.

The bottom line? Jensen had been setting himself up for anger with his limited response capability to his experience of fear. He knew only to blame and control. He was not then able or willing to take the personal risks of searching inside himself for other, more heroic choices.

Jensen can still blame and control, but he can also make several more effective choices and decisions about himself, his own life, and what to do with it. Most important for Jensen's growing ability to avoid setting himself up for anger is his new willingness to take personal risks with the way others might see him.

Since Jensen now experiences more control in his own life, he no longer needs to attempt to control Marion's, or to blame

anger avoidance toolkit

---

the off button

Increase your response capability:

SWITCH IT OFF!

If there is something you regularly do, see, or hear that always hits your anger button—and you really don't have to do, see, or hear it—then hit the off button. Switch it off or out. If you can't switch it off or out, walk away!

Then do, see, or hear something else. Let something else into your experience that doesn't make you feel angry; try letting something in that makes you feel good.

---

the difference maker

Increase your response capability:

DO SOMETHING DIFFERENT!

David exercised the greatest power we humans have: the power to choose to do things differently. David learned how to change the emotional experience of his anger by doing something different in response to one of the daily events that triggered it. The result was that he also transformed his experience of the rest of his day, at work and with his family.

---

the risk taker

Increase your response capability:

TAKE RISKS WITH YOURSELF!

Jensen's need to blame and control his wife reduced as he assumed more control over and responsibility for his own life. That began to happen when Jensen became willing to take personal risks with the judgements others might make about him—especially his friends. His response capability (or response-ability) began to increase, not only in his marital relationship, but also in other areas of his life.

---

her when things go wrong. Once Jensen learned how to use "the risk taker," he was able to make different choices, and life for him and Marion became safer and richer.

These three stories—"The Off Button," "The Difference Maker," and "The Risk Taker"—all have something useful to say about how we often set ourselves up to get angry, and what we can do to prevent that. They each offer different anger-avoidance tools, which are summarized on page 139.

why not try it yourself today?

Why not try doing something quite different, or taking a risk by exposing something about your secret emotional life to a trusted friend or buddy? You might be surprised at the response you get.

Again, as with every strategy in this book, if you're not sure you quite understand or can do these tasks alone, ask for help from a counselor.

releasing your anger

When angry, count four; when very angry, swear.

— Mark Twain

As we shall explore further in Chapter 14, anger is not only emotion, it is energy.[1] Most men and women know intuitively that the best and fastest way to get anger "out of your system" is to work it off. In this chapter, we're going to get you to set yourself up with some healthy and practical ways of working off your anger. These will be useful as stand-alone strategies for dealing with some lower-level anger episodes. They will also be very important later, as components of a more comprehensive and practical system for controlling your anger. I call them anger release options or AROs.

what is an anger release option?

Simply, an ARO is any activity that causes energy to be expended from the body. The *release of anger energy* should not be confused with the *expression of anger*, which is a communication exercise. Whatever you currently do, or could do if you so choose, is a potential ARO—*if it expends energy*. Let me explain.

If I want you to succeed in dealing with your anger, I cannot afford to make any assumptions about your skills or resources. And, unlike the case with my clients, I do not have the opportunity to meet with you and explore your resources in person. Instead, I have to use these pages to guide you through the task of exploring your own interests, skills, activities, and resources for practical options that you can use as AROs. Your best AROs, in other words, either exist already in your own lifestyle and immediate environment, or can be found and recruited.

Many common activities are potential AROs. Walking is one that most able people can use; the fast walk (or power walk) is ideal for expending the intense energy buildup that most people experience during angry episodes. Weightlifting, throwing, running, and aerobic exercise are all effective, active ways of expending anger energy.

Passive pursuits work for some people. They include music, reading, and similar relaxing kinds of pastimes. These operate on the basis of energy dissipation, the old distraction idea—"give it time and it will go away." It is important to know that these are usually slow to work and can often leave the person "stewing" rather than exhausted.

Many people will attempt to "get control" by smoking, drinking (alcoholic or nonalcoholic beverages), or eating. The implicit direction of energy with these is inward.[2] Mostly, these measures tend to "bury" anger superficially and temporarily, thereby *adding* to the accumulated store. Please remember that you are pouring energy *into* the body when you consume food or drink (except for water) or other mood-altering substances, such as nicotine. When you are angry, you need to exhaust your energy, *not* take in more. Therefore, these activities are *not* among the recommended AROs.

Another activity to avoid when you are angry is driving. As tempting as it may be to leap into your car and floor it around the freeways or across the country roads while you burn off steam, doing so when your emotions are out of control endangers you and others. *Do not attempt to operate a vehicle (or other heavy machinery) when under the influence of your anger.*

aros are all around you

When I was a kid, I was obsessed with rafts. With other kids, I would build rafts from empty five-gallon kerosene cans, rusty corrugated iron, old floorboards—anything we could scavenge. We'd shoot the rapids on our state-of-the-art craft, or we'd turn them into pirate ships and invade the coast, or we'd just cruise up and down the river. They never survived more than one or two trips down the rapids. As for the crew, we were lucky to have survived the shipwrecks!

The thing about rafts is they can be built from just about anything that floats or that can be assisted to float. The material is usually just lying around or being used for some other, less adventurous purpose. There is only one criterion for building a raft: It must keep you afloat in rough water and rapids.

Rafts can be cobbled together with all sorts of bits and pieces. So can your raft of AROs. But there are two criteria for AROs: They must stay afloat (be available to you) in emotional rough water and rapids, and they should burn up energy—quickly.

Just sit alone quietly for ten to fifteen minutes and review your past life, your present lifestyle, your circumstances (location, environment, age, health and fitness), and your available resources. You should focus your attention on any activities you have done, still do, or might consider doing that consume or expend significant levels of energy.

On a sheet of paper, write them all down, even the wildest ideas—perhaps excluding whale wrestling!

Maybe you did weight training when you were a teenager, excelled at cross-country running in school, rode a surfboard, climbed mountains, or just walked a lot.

What about activities and challenges you have fantasized about in your imagination but never considered in reality? Maybe you have always wanted to ride a mountain bike, try rollerblading, shoot basketball, or just jog.

Maybe you have watched those wheelchair athletes and

wondered how they get so fit and strong. Maybe you just enjoy walking fast (or working your chair) around suburban streets in the cool night air. Or, maybe you have fantasized about hiking that mountain just outside of town.

You can recruit any of these activities as AROs. Dozens of others exist in or around your daily life. As long as they use up energy, they qualify. All you need do is choose them and use them—as your personal anger release options.

building a raft of aros

A good rule of thumb is to keep AROs simple. If you are in a high-level anger episode, the last thing you need is to have to change clothes, organize transportation, or stand in line at a gym door waiting for opening time. The more sophisticated activities might be okay at lower levels, but you need activities you can do immediately and with minimum fuss at higher levels of anger.

When considering a particular activity as a potential ARO, you should think about the resources and information you might need.

Depending on the particular activity, you need to pay attention to basic things like running shoes, sweat suits, and water bottles, as well as to more specialized things like gym memberships, rollerblades, access to basketball courts, and so on. And make sure you climbers have a mountain nearby!

The information you need might include operating hours of the swimming pool or gym, location of bike rides and walks, and so on. It will help you make it all happen if you write up a brief schedule for commencement of your AROs (e.g., enrolling at a gym, checking out pool times).

Some activities that make effective AROs appear in the table titled "ARO Examples," below. Notice how, apart from weight training or working out in a gym, most are low-cost, low-resource activities. Of course, you can do things like jogging, running, fast walking, skipping, or calisthenics just about anywhere, any time, and at a moment's notice.

Next, immediately following the "ARO Examples" table, you will find a blank form titled "My AROs." In the left-hand column, enter the activities that you have selected as AROs. Use a separate box for each entry. In the corresponding box in the right-hand column, fill in the resources and information you need in order to do the activity (the "ARO Examples" table should help with that).

Once you've completed the entries in both columns of "My AROs," you'll have a personal raft of AROs from which to select next time you get angry.

Now there's one more important thing to do. Your partner is going to get pretty confused and angry when you start walking out instead of dealing with the issue. It is important to explain what you are going to do and when you will be back. (We'll talk about this again later.) Why not make a copy of your raft of AROs for your partner? That way, people will know what to expect, and will feel included in your program. Better still, post it on the fridge so the whole family will know you are serious about releasing your anger without affecting or harming them.

Yes! Anger release *can be* as easy as that.

Stunning, isn't it, to think that our ability to release anger energy safely—and thereby avoid risking harm or damage—is right there inside us. We just have to decide and do it.

cautions

- If you are inactive now, or have doubts about your level of health and fitness, see your doctor for a physical checkup.

- Without expert advice, do not attempt activities that require new skills or training.

- Consider the practical viability of the activity as an ARO. Is it something you can do at a moment's notice, close to home or work or anywhere else you are likely to have an anger episode?

– Finally, you need to balance your preference with your finances! Stress triggers anger. Don't make more stress for yourself by choosing AROs that are going to cost more money than you can afford.

Now build your own raft of AROs, using the examples and the form provided below, and adding your own.

This is a good time to get your fitness level checked out. Get advice from your doctor or a qualified coach at a local gym if you have any doubt about your ability to do the AROs you've selected. You don't have to say why you're starting these new activities; just say it's time to change your lifestyle. Well, that's true, isn't it?

aro examples

activity	resources and information
Jogging	You need running shoes, sweat suit or shorts, and water bottle. Your rapid expenditure of energy through hard jogging will leave your body drained of tension and quite tired.
Weight Training	Find a local gym with a qualified trainer or class. You need to line up your membership now so that when you're angry, you know where to go and what to do. Repetitions and weights can be adjusted to maximize energy consumption.
Aerobic Exercise	Find a local gym and a regular class. Get your own audiotape or videotape for use when angry. This is another great energy expender.
Calisthenics	Push ups, sit-ups, jumping jacks, and squats are all great energy users. No special resources needed—just a floor and some time.
Lap or Speed Swimming	If you have a backyard pool big enough to swim in, this activity is a winner for rapid energy expenditure. If you don't have your own pool, join a gym or inquire at the local city-operated pool about hours designated for adult lap swimming.

my aros

activity	resources and information

chapter nine

controlling your anger

It's my rule never to lose my temper
Until it would be detrimental to keep it.

— Sean O'Casey[1]

There is a particular power tool in my shed
that, when correctly operated (remember the old saying, "the
right tool for the right job"), has something that sets it apart
from other power tools. It is my power saw—and it always
sounds so angry! I know it can be dangerous, and I pride
myself on my (usual) commitment to safe practices and procedures. I respect the awesome power and potential of my saw. I
also know that its power and potential are the main reasons for
having it. I admit to a healthy fear of my power saw, but when I
am using it, I never want it to stop doing what it does best—
cutting things in two. At the same time, I don't want an accident: an injury or an outcome that was never intended.

Do you use a power saw? If you do, have you ever noticed
that once you have passed a certain point, you cannot safely
back out of a cut while the saw is still going? That threshold,
for most saws, is passed once the full circumference of the saw
(including its tailing edge) is committed to the cut. If you do
try to back out, the saw sounds angrier than ever. Safe practice
is to stop the saw and carefully take it out.

anger is like a power saw

It is my experience that real anger—my own and that of others—is a bit like a power saw committed to the cut. It is very hard to back out once your tailing edge is in, so you have to switch it off before you can extract it from the job. Unlike the saw, the deeper your anger, the harder it is to switch it off and extract yourself from the scene. Like the saw, once you lose control of anger, it can run rampant and wreak havoc.[2]

If I am going to undertake a big and difficult cutting job, I have some strategies to make the job safer, easier, and more predictable; I minimize the risk of losing control and doing damage. I figure if it is smart to have precautions for my power saw, it might be smart to have precautions for my anger.

I am human; there will be times and circumstances in which I will get angry. But I do not want a dangerous incident. I cannot afford to lose control—nor can my family afford for me to. I need a strategy that will help me make sure harm does not happen. I need a system for controlling my anger.

This reminds me of Rajid, the underworld figure to whom I introduced you in Chapter 3. You might recall that Rajid was about to give evidence that would convict someone of murder. His whole life he had tried to live by one simple rule: Don't get scared; get control! But by the time he was referred to me, there were few areas of his life still under his control, and he was more often losing control of his anger.

rajid's story continues

When Rajid and I met for our first session, he was panic-stricken by his fear of losing control. He feared that one of his erstwhile associates in crime would turn up on his doorstep to silence him. He was worried for his girlfriend's life, for that of their child, and for his own. Specifically, he was anxious that if he lost control in a situation of serious threat, he might not be able to think clearly and protect them. He also feared that he might kill or maim his assailant and find himself back inside. Prison meant many things for Rajid, including the threat of solitary confinement—his sister's closet all over again.

"The cops want it both ways," said Rajid of the police. "They want my evidence to nail the bastard who wasted M, and they want me inside again. But they don't want me inside 'til after the trial—my life's at greater risk inside than outside. No Rajid, no evidence, no conviction; simple as that."

"So what's the problem?" I don't think I had ever sounded so naïve.

"Shit! For a counselor, you don't know much. All they've got to do is get me to lose control, get mad, and do someone. Then they'll hang one on me—*after* the murder trial. Once I've given my evidence, I've got no leverage. You get it?"

I got it!

By session six, Rajid and I were able to confront the practical issues of his current predicament—what to do with those anger episodes that might occur when he felt threatened or attacked. Rajid had done great work on his BioScan; in fact, his girlfriend said he was like a new man. But both of them were still scared of the angry episode that might overtake him if someone turned up to "negotiate" with him, or if a cop tried to entrap him. Rajid wanted something more—a backstop or insurance policy of some kind.

What Rajid needed was some internal, reliable, and automatic system for recognizing his anger and dealing with it effectively—even under threat. There were three specific aids he was looking for:

1. He needed some way of knowing just how angry he was—how close he was to losing control.

2. He needed to have some alternative choices and actions available to him *consciously*—before losing control.

3. He needed some physical way of "coming down" again, of expelling all that anger energy from his body—harmlessly.

If Rajid could have such a system, he knew he would be better placed to make different choices, take alternative actions, that would reduce the risks for everyone involved. Certainly, Rajid lived a hazardous life in a criminal world that few of us would approve of and most of us would condemn. Yet what was true of his need for an effective system of anger control is just as true of many other men who struggle with their anger. Few men get to do the emotional work that my clients do and that you did in Chapters 5 and 6. Rajid did that work really well. I like to think that the work he did with me had something to do with his success in quitting the underworld and building a legitimate business for himself and his family.[3] Still, he felt he needed a fallback in case he found himself at risk of losing it again in future.

practical systems for anger control

After doing a BioScan and the emotional work associated with it, all of my clients work with me to develop a practical system for anger control. Few of them report needing it in the long term, but they appreciate the added security of knowing it is there. I guess they integrate it so well into their lives that they cease to see it as a separate system.

First, let's get clear about what a practical system for anger control will *not* do for you. It will *not* quickly heal or resolve the lifetime of accumulated emotional stuff that might be driving your anger. Anger is an emotion that you cannot resolve without doing the emotionally demanding work that we did in Chapters 5 and 6. Just as you cannot resolve practical issues with emotional methods alone, so you cannot resolve emotional issues with practical methods alone. It is a classic case of needing the right tool for the right job.[4]

Second, anger control is not an interpersonal communication tool. Indeed, as you will see, the system you develop with this book is highly personal, stays inside you, and has nothing really to do with anyone else. There are heaps of communication programs, books, and tapes available. It is quite likely that using one of them will help improve interpersonal communication in your relationships and family life. Shop around, or ask your nearest community service agency or library for recommendations.

Finally, a practical system for anger control depends for its success upon your own internal and external resources. (You will learn what I mean by those terms in the following chapters.) Thus, you cannot give it to somebody else to look after or operate for you. Nobody else can build the system for you, nor can you get any of the parts you need from anyone else— because they simply do not have them. Like your BioScan, this one comes from you.

So that is what a practical system for anger control won't do. Now let's talk about what it *will* do for you.

I said above that anger control is not an interpersonal communication tool, and that's true. But it is an *intrapersonal*, or internal, communication tool. The anger-control system you will learn in Chapters 10 to 13 is really a system of communicating with yourself. Not only will you use your thoughts and (internal) "self-talk," but also the feedback signals you get from your body, your emotions, and your behavior.

To be effective, a practical system for anger control must have these features:

1. An accessible and comprehensive *log* of anger signals.

2. A reliable way of *reading* your anger signals to gauge your *anger level*.

3. A menu of *strategic choices* for action at your different anger levels.

4. An on-paper *monitor* of the system that mirrors outside yourself the communication system being set up inside. You can use it as a learning aid and as a reminder, and you can modify it as you go.

The monitor reminds you about what is happening with your anger and what you can and need to do about it at different levels. I developed the prototype of this system for Rajid a few years ago. With affection and reverence, I named it PAM— personal anger monitor. You will see what PAM looks like in Chapter 13.

The basic tool PAM uses is your log of what I call "progressive anger signals," so called because they relate to different *levels* of rising anger.

So what are anger signals? That question is covered in the next chapter.

recognizing your anger signals

Know thyself.

— Inscribed on the temple of Apollo at Delphi

Rajid needed a system for controlling his anger, his own personal signal system and anger monitor that would prompt him to make well-timed behavior choices that would be safer than the limited options he felt stuck with.

Now, some people might say, "Hell! What's wrong with the bloke? Why can't he be responsible and just choose not to lose control when he's angry?" And that's a fair question—from someone who has never lost it, or who has forgotten what it was like to lose it. Me? I understood exactly what Rajid was looking for—he wanted a railway signal box that would tell him in advance when his anger train was about to run him over as well as a set of railway points that would send the train off safely in another direction.

To help Rajid create such a system, I had to register the most important clue, which Rajid himself had given me—his rule of life: "Don't get scared; get control!"

You need to understand what he meant by "control." He had to control himself; that was true. More important, as Rajid saw it, he had to control any situation he was in or might get into. If he didn't, then he feared he might be scared. If he was scared, that would show—and then he would be in deep trouble. He had known that much all his life!

Masculine culture in our society supports Rajid's view: "Real men don't show they're hurt, and they don't show they're scared." Men learn early that they must control their feelings—especially pain and fear. A colleague of mine has suggested to me his theory that when we lose control of the situation we are in, we lose control of our feelings, too. It is as though we then have to impose some other sort of control over ourselves and others to compensate—to make it look as if we are in control, even when we are not. That's where anger comes to the rescue—fuelled by all that accumulated, unexpressed pain and fear.

rajid's anger signals

If Rajid could have a conscious set of signals that would tell him when he was starting down the old anger track, maybe he could do something about it *before* he lost control and became violent. The only place such a system could come from was inside Rajid himself. We knew he didn't have a conscious set of signals. The question was whether he had any *unconscious* signals we could bring to consciousness and employ.

Rajid agreed we should try to find out.

I led Rajid into a state of deep relaxation. In that state, a person is able to focus on all his senses and internal awareness. Unlike the hypnotic state, deep relaxation leaves the person fully conscious and in control of the experience. While in that state, I had Rajid "revisit" the last time he recalled being out of control—not necessarily angry, just not in control. I asked him to find some recent event or experience that really raised his anxiety level. He picked the day his girlfriend Moira drove him to town.

Rajid couldn't cope with being a passenger in a car when anyone else was driving. Either Rajid drove or he didn't get in—simple as that. But he was late for reporting to his local police station (a condition of his current bail order), and he had broken his hand, which was plastered and slung. Their car was a manual. You needed two hands to drive it—especially if you were intending to pull up at the police station. There was no choice: Moira had to drive! Rajid's anxiety level went through the roof that day as Moira drove him into town. Then he started getting angry—at Moira, at the cops, at his hand, and at himself.

So, in my office, while Rajid was in a relaxed state, yet still in touch with his anxiety and anger, I quietly asked him some important questions:

Frank: Rajid, stay in touch there and stay relaxed as well. Now, what's starting to happen around your body as you move from being anxious to getting angry?

Rajid: Well, I am getting very tense in my gut for a start. My face feels hard and I'm starting to sweat. And my legs...they start shaking.

Frank: Your head and face are starting to go red, Rajid. Is that what happens when you get angry?

Rajid: Moira says that, too. I know it feels like they might be going red. I mean, I can't see them, unless there's a mirror or a reflective window. But I can feel the burning. My face is hard and my head and face feel hot. And, shit, you know what else, Frank? I can feel the veins at the side of my head [temples] and forehead starting to swell and "pop."

Frank: Anything else, about your body, I mean?

Rajid: Yeah, there is—and it happens often when I'm getting so angry and I'm losing it...you know...that control. It's just...going! I'm going....

Frank: Sorry Rajid, I don't understand; is that a physical thing, or...?

Rajid: Well...it's like...I mean, I'm in the car this time... but it happens a lot when I'm angry. I feel off-balance, dizzy somehow...like I'll fall over if it gets any worse or I don't get control of this. But it's weird. As I get dizzy, I also feel—uh— supercharged. Yeah, that's right—I start to feel supercharged. Then I'm ready to fight, and I don't give a shit! I...I just don't care anymore....

Frank: Okay, good. I don't know if you're aware of this, but you are also starting to talk very loudly, and in short bursts....

Rajid: Yeah, yeah. I can hear myself. You don't have to tell me.

Frank: Sorry! What else are you doing now—you know, like movement and actions, maybe?

Rajid: Okay, I'm aware that my shoulders start to bunch and my fists clench. And as I get angrier—going up, you might say—I am really wanting to pace around. That's what I do if I'm standing.

Frank: Rajid, what are you feeling emotionally now? You know what I mean—like some of those feelings we went through in the last few sessions?

Rajid: That's still kinda hard...there's a lot of stuff churning round between my head and my guts. In fact, that's what it's like...like a freeway jammed up with traffic wanting to go every fuckin' where except where I'm going. I'm scared...you know? But I don't get scared—that's the rule—at least it used to be till you stuck your nose in!

Frank: Hey, man! You came looking for me, not vice versa. Still, I know what you mean, so what's going on with your feelings now?

Rajid: Well, it's the closet again now....

Frank: Hang on, first we're bumper-to-bumper on a freeway, now we're in your sister's closet? You sure move around a lot....

Rajid: Yeah, well, that's how it is in here. The thing is not to let them take you—that's why I live by the rule "don't get scared, get control!" But what's happening is I'm losing it again, and the only way to stop 'em is to fight back, give 'em shit, do whatever, but don't let 'em think they've won...especially the cops....

When I brought Rajid out of his deep relaxation state, he was visibly shaken by the number and range of signals he had been able to identify. Have a look back over our interview segment and see if you recognize any of Rajid's anger signals personally. Do you experience any of them when you get angry?

Notice especially that Rajid was not asked to recall specifically an anger episode, but *any* event in which he had no control. Notice how his acute anxiety—another word for fear—led him straight down the track to his anger. Does that happen to you? Does your fear get squashed and replaced by anger? For a man, fear is not okay the way anger is okay. Yet, it's such a common trigger for anger—that is what makes it such a reliable signal for anger!

Now look at the interview segment again and notice how, in response to my different questions, Rajid first describes the things he notices happening to or in his body. Then he reports the things he does, or feels impelled to do. Last, he reports the inner, emotional feelings he experiences. So Rajid now had consciously available three different sets of telltale signals to his anger.[1]

three types of anger signals

Physical signals—the things our bodies do involuntarily

Behavioral signals—the things we do; our actions and words

Emotional signals—the things our emotions do; our feelings

Let's extract Rajid's signals from the conversation above and have a look at them. See if you recognize any of them from your own anger episodes.

You might start recalling some of the things your own body does or that you experience yourself doing and feeling when you start getting angry, and also as your anger continues to build. These are *your* anger signals. You might not have been conscious of them as individual signals in the past, but as you read on there will be more examples—all taken from

rajid's anger signals

physical (around the body)	behavioral (actions and words)	emotional (feelings)
Gut tensing up	Starts talking loudly and in short bursts	Feels churned up
Face feeling hard		Feels the flow of "traffic" (people, events, or things) goes against him
Head and face going red	Bunching shoulders	
Body sweating	Clenching and unclenching fists	
Legs shaking and trembling	Pacing around	Starts to feel scared; experiences "emotional memories" of sister's closet
Veins in temples and forehead swelling or "popping"		Feels is losing control and must fight back to prevent that
Feels off-balance and dizzy		Feels ready to fight back—"can't let them win"
Body feels super-charged (i.e., bursting with energy and strength)		Doesn't care anymore

the experiences of other men. Make notes of any you recognize in yourself.

Let's talk about these three general types of anger signals in some detail.

physical signals

This group of signals includes all of the things we experience our body doing from the first stages of anger right through to that stage when we seem to have lost control. Rajid's is one sample of physical signals; you will find more in "Other Men's Signals," below.

Physical signals include things like perspiration, (involuntarily) trembling or shaking limbs, hot skin flushes, physical tension (in abdomen, chest, or muscles), rapid and louder heartbeat, swollen veins (especially around the temples). Some physical signals occur at different levels of intensity as our anger builds up. Some occur specifically at higher levels of anger, while others are more commonly associated with onset and early stages.

Many physical signals are the physiological or neurological consequences of earlier signals. For example, significant tremors or shaking of upper limbs result directly from increased tension in the body. The common sequence is an increased tension at lower anger levels, followed by tremors or shaking at higher levels. Another example is the common experience of increased and louder heartbeat at the middle stage of anger arousal (as blood pressure increases), followed by a noticeable swelling of the temporal (or other) blood vessels.

The behavioral and emotional events and signals we experience when angry can be overwhelming. To be able to make sound choices about our actions when we get angry, we first need to understand and come to terms with the spiraling physical escalation of anger.[2] The best way to start doing that is to learn to *consciously recognize* our physical anger signals, the sequence in which they occur, and the level of anger we have reached at the time.

behavioral signals

This group of signals includes all of the things we do both consciously and unconsciously, which some people recognize as *angry body language*. Some people start to pace up and down. Some clench and unclench their fists. Some start yelling; others reduce their speech volume to a whisper (both of which are often experienced by the other person as controlling behaviors). Then there are the palm thumpers, the table bangers, and the door slammers. Some of us start to huff and puff, some clench teeth, point fingers, and jab the air. You know them—or some of them. There are thousands of these behavioral signals to anger.

Have you seen or heard other people do these behaviors when they were angry? Of course you have! Rajid's signals are but one example; you'll find more in "Other Men's Signals," below.

The question is, which behaviors do *you* do when *you* are angry?

If you don't know what you do when you are angry, you need to find out. And you need to know roughly how angry you are when you start to do those typical things.

Why?

Because our behaviors—what we do—seem to have a significant impact upon our physical and emotional systems and, therefore, upon the rate of escalation and intensity of anger. For example, if you pace quickly, you may increase your heart rate, blood pressure, and the swelling of your blood vessels. If you get short of breath and start yelling a lot, you will increase your respiratory difficulty and discomfort, thereby increasing your emotional state of agitation and anger. If you thump the palms of your hands on tabletops or walls as your anger level climbs through your threshold, you are much more likely to *feel* violent. You want to hit *someone*—simply because you now feel driven to do more than just hit *something*. Whether the person around you is the actual object of your anger, or just an available human target, the risk of your doing serious harm to that person now becomes extreme.

You don't believe me?

How many times have you, or someone you know, harmed a partner, child, or friend, only to cry remorsefully and bitterly afterwards, "I didn't mean to harm her—I really didn't!! I just don't know what came over me."

There are dozens more of these behavioral impacts upon your physical and emotional signals—the unintended, uncontrolled physical and emotional outcomes of what you actually *do* when you are angry.

The point is that when you *know* what you do, you can identify your behavioral signals. When you can identify your behavioral signals, you can make behavioral choices: You can begin to choose what you do *before* you go through your control threshold. When you can choose your behavior, you can limit the effects of those inter-system impacts. The exciting part is that you can now start to have some conscious control over many of those involuntary physical effects that previously you were not even aware of and much less able to control. Just imagine the real power you will have over your anger—the only power that really counts here—once you can start to control the choices you make about what you actually do when you are angry.

emotional signals

Here we need to recap a little.

Remember that I have said previously that anger is an internal emotional experience and that men who have a serious problem with anger tend to experience their anger intensely. I have also said that we get angry when we experience what can be called an assault upon the self and that our earliest experiences of assaults upon the self often leave the most enduring imprints on our "emotional memories," later to be reproduced in our adult intimate relationships.

Rajid's childhood closet experience was one of those assaults upon the self; the terror of being locked in conflicted with the rule that boys are tough—they don't tell and they don't get scared. So he had to deny his fear and his need to tell; he had to bury them down deep where nobody would see. You can see shades of that experience repeated in Rajid's present emotional signals for anger.

In this book, we cannot reproduce conversations with all my clients as we have done with Rajid's. But when you read the profiles of those men whose anger signals appear below, in "Other Men's Signals," you will notice how their emotional signals also seem to reflect some earlier emotional experience.

So it's right now, in the adult present, where it all happens—over and over. The anger we are displaying now towards our partners is loaded (primed) with an accumulation of anger against a lifetime of assaults upon the self. Those assaults squash and bury deep inside some really important emotional parts and sensory potentials, often rejected as too feminine for real men. That rejection and inner burial is what is meant by "self-alienation." For some of us that alienation is deeper, more total, than for others. The greater our level of self-alienation, the more threatening the present anger-arousing event, the less we are in control, and the more angry we feel.

This is a most-important observation and bears repeating: *The more we "lose it," the less we feel in control, and the more angry we become.*

The vicious cycle of anger just keeps on turning, around and around. Frustrated by the consequent loss of control over our lives, we become angry most of all at ourselves.

Why?

As every man is brought up to believe, control over ourselves, over the situations we find ourselves in, and over our own lives is the minimum requirement for all that is meant, socially and culturally, by "manhood." To lose control is the ultimate fear.

Sadly, self-control and conquest, rather than self-awareness and acceptance, are the benchmarks for success as a man. They are the twin pivots around which turns our manhood. From those same pivots, we cast out the unspoken, the feminine, the less-than-manly parts of our selfhoods. Ignorance is indeed fear—since so much of ourselves is lost to our awareness, there is so much of ourselves to fear. That is the most painful cost of our alienation.

The vicious cycle of lost control ➡ fear ➡ anger ➡ more lost control is at the heart of the emotion of anger for men. Here we are not speaking of power or control over others; here we speak specifically of *lost power and control over ourselves.* It is not difficult to understand why anger has been described so often as the most complex emotion of them all!

The good news is this: The whole grab bag of feelings mixed up in anger tends to come to the surface as we get angry. Like those physical and behavioral signals we have talked about, you probably have not been aware of those feelings as discrete emotions until now.

Recall the last time you were seriously angry. Apart from the aggressive burst of energy, can you remember the initial fear or threat of potential harm (not necessarily physical injury) that you felt? Were you scared of what you might do to yourself, to someone else, or to your property or home? As your anger ballooned up from inside, can you touch again that sense of losing control over what was happening to you, or the events around you, or yourself? What did you want to do? Did you start blaming someone in particular or just "everybody"? Did you want to fight or flee? Did you find yourself wishing "it" away? Did you feel driven to lash out, to smash, or to injure? Did you feel as though something hot and volcanic was erupting, or was it more like cold steel or ice? Was there a numbing inside, or was there a creeping need to hurt someone?

It is probably difficult for you to recall these feelings without experiencing even more feelings of embarrassment, shame, or guilt. In fact, it may take more than a little personal courage to complete the task that is coming up shortly.

other men's signals

fabian's story

Fabian is a security officer with a major international hotel chain. But life and work were not always so safe or "respectable" for Fabian, who immigrated from Europe as a child with his family. He was brought up in a tough Melbourne suburban environment and was seriously victimized at school

fabian's anger signals

physical (around the body)	behavioral (actions and words)	emotional (feelings)
Abdominal heat erupting	Doing uncontrolled and vicious things	Anger erupting like a volcano
Heat brewing in stomach	"Don't hit women rule" clicking on	Fear (of men) fading out
Energy rush developing		
Previous signals going numb	Speech becoming tightly controlled	
Eyes watering		
Muscles tightening		
Lips drying		
Slight body shaking		
Slight general tension developing		

as a "wog." He grew very tough after a major gang-violence episode during his early teens, in which his friend was seriously beaten and Fabian was unable to help. Vowing never to be put in such a position again, he began serious weight training and martial arts training. He became a "successful" hotel and nightclub bouncer before he was twenty-one.

It was in a nightclub where his anger (as opposed to strategic violence) first surfaced as a problem, when he began losing control with patrons he was supposed to be ejecting from the premises. What brought Fabian to me was his loss of control at home with his girlfriend. He was smashing glasses and dishes, punching walls, and destroying furniture in angry episodes. No emotional softy, Fabian presented to me with a broken hand and a near-broken heart. Someone who had attended one of my seminars referred him.

Fabian's signals made sense to him—he recognized them from his experience of his own anger. They might not make sense to you. Nor should they necessarily: They're not your signals. If you have signals like Fabian's, you may well know them by different names and descriptions. This is especially true of behavioral and emotional signals. Notice Fabian's "don't hit women" rule. You might expect that to be clicking off instead of on. But for Fabian, that's not how it is: When he gets angry, he quickly moves into a fighting style and stance that comes from his own unique background. There are some rules about that stance that seem to travel with him into his anger, at least temporarily: One of these is "you don't hit women." You will see in the next chapter how this too can change.

kevin's story

Kevin operates a fast-food outlet in partnership with his wife, Rosemary. Their marriage of twenty-three years was about to collapse under the strain of increased tension and fighting. Rosemary had had enough of living in chronic fear and risk of

Kevin's drinking, anger, and violence. It soon came out that Kevin had lived most of his life with guilt and self-loathing. It started way back with his alcoholic, angry, and abusive father, who beat Kevin and his brothers, as well as their mother, for most of Kevin's childhood. Kevin was his alcoholic and violent father's favorite, and he loved him in return, hence the guilt and self-loathing that drove his anger. To calm the one, he first had to heal the other. Unlike his father, Kevin discovered he couldn't hide in a bottle, that he needed to confront himself.

Notice how Kevin has a more detailed inventory of anger signals. Like Fabian, these are things that he feels deeply ashamed of. But since they happen every time he gets angry, he's saying to himself, "Well, I don't have to like them, much

kevin's anger signals

physical (around the body)	behavioral (actions and words)	emotional (feelings)
Frothing at the mouth	Voice rising	Guts "tied in knots"
Voice quivering	Yelling	Feeling upset
Quivering and shaking	Standing "nose-to-nose"	Feeling driven to smash opponent in the mouth
Getting tense	Standing up	
Getting hot	Closing/opening fists	Feeling hated by the world
Sweat dripping off brow	Bracing legs	
Body tensing more	Screaming	
Hair on neck standing up	Striking	
	Pacing and moving	
	Smashing walls or car	

less be proud of them, but if they tell me something about my anger and I can use them as information to help me control it, well, why not?" Notice also how Kevin has many more behavioral signals: He works in a fast-food outlet where getting things done fast while attending to customers, employees, and events around the ovens and counters demands a wide variety of actions and responses.

michael's story

Michael, a bricklayer in his early twenties, was referred by his psychiatrist. Michael had been sexually abused several times by three different men in his childhood, but never had been able to disclose these incidents to parents or anyone else until now. Recently detoxed (he had abused himself with drugs and alcohol), Michael revealed that he had been violent with his live-in

michael's anger signals

physical (around the body)	behavioral (actions and words)	emotional (feelings)
Heart beating faster and louder	Yelling and screaming	Feeling urge to break something
	Balling his fists	
Breath getting short		
	Breaking something or hitting someone with fist, hand, or object	
Head and ears getting hot		
Shoulders and chest getting tight		
Getting hotter		
Arms and hands shaking		
Tension and tightness increasing		

girlfriend, pushing her around and slapping her, causing a bloody nose. Before I could see Michael, his girlfriend's safety had to be guaranteed. Michael moved back to his parents' home to minimize her risk of harm. The psychiatrist was also treating Michael with medication for depression.

Like Fabian, Michael has more physical signals than behavioral or emotional ones. Michael is a bricklayer whose everyday life is full of physical awareness and prompts. He and Fabian (a security officer) have physical occupations that demand a greater awareness of physical reflexes, fitness, and strength. I guess that's why they are both very aware of their physical signals.

Fabian, Kevin, and Michael are fictitious names for three ordinary Australian men who live hard, work hard, and play hard. They are competitive in the gym, on the field, or on the court. They are not known to each other or to any other of my clients. About the only thing they had in common was their desperate determination to control their anger and stop its violent outcomes. Anger was running and ruining their lives. It was also creating hell for those around them, doing harm and putting lives at risk.

Each of these men had completed with me the emotional work described in Chapters 5 and 6 before starting formally on the task of identifying his anger signals. They all had reported feeling much stronger since freeing themselves to know, own, and express their emotional feelings.

Fabian, Kevin, and Michael all confirmed that the emotional work we did together turned their lives around and freed them to grow and succeed. They all reckon it was the "heart" work from Part II of this book that made it possible for them to go on to this "head" task and make sense of it. But it was the process of becoming conscious of and recognizing their physical, behavioral, and emotional signals to anger that finally gave them something they'd never had before—the ability to know, own, and direct their anger so they never needed to lose control again. You can achieve the same results. So now it is your turn to identify your own anger signals. Let's do it!

identify your anger signals

what you need for this task

To identify and list your anger signals, you need only this book and three other things:

1. About one hour to yourself (and no one else!) in a quiet place.

2. Some paper and a pen or pencil.

3. Your memory of what happened to your body, your behavior, and your emotions as you climbed through your anger levels last time you got seriously angry.

what the task is about

I am not asking you to recall the last half dozen times you got annoyed at someone or something; I am asking you to recall to conscious experience the last time you were so angry that you lost control. Maybe you threw things, smashed things, punched walls or furniture, drove your car like a maniac, hit someone—*that* is the time I am asking you to recall—just as if you were recalling a very dramatic movie that seemed to drag you into the scenes on the screen. What did you hear, see, and feel your body, your behavior, and your emotions doing? These are your physical, behavioral, and emotional signals to your anger.

Do not be tempted to discount one of your signals because it seems trivial, commonplace, or unimportant. For example, if you sweat when you are angry, but you sweat normally anyway, don't discount it by saying to yourself, "Well, I sweat easily, especially under pressure, so I won't write that down." It is important that you write down everything that your body does, that you do, and that your emotions do as you get angry. What we are trying to build here is a raw list of all the things that happen to you when you get angry.

use all the examples in this chapter

Review the section "Other Men's Signals," above. As well as illustrating what I mean by "anger signals," you will be reassured that other men have experiences similar to you when they are angry. If you recognize any of your own signals in their lists, write them down.

give yourself time and space

Do not attempt this exercise until you can give yourself the time (at least one hour) and space to do so—on your own and with no interruptions.

here's how to relax

If you intend to use a relaxation tape, that's okay, but be warned: Some relaxation programs use guided imagery to produce a warm, comfortable, and peaceful experience. That is not going to help you recall your anger!

Just sit back, close your eyes, and take a deep breath through your nose; hold it for three seconds, and then let it out through your mouth—pursing your lips. Repeat three to five times.

Then let your breathing slow down, becoming shallow, even, and regular.

Now mentally go through all your body parts progressively (as though you were doing an inventory), noticing and discharging any tension in them, relaxing them as you go. Start with your head and neck, move to your shoulders, upper and lower arms and hands, chest and mid-back, abdomen and lower back, hips, upper and lower legs, finishing with your ankles and feet. The trick is to "command" the tension to drain away and your body parts to relax, one by one. Most important is to "command" each part as you breathe *out*—not as you breathe in.

recall your last serious anger episode

1. When you feel relaxed, recall your last serious anger episode.

Keep yourself detached and relaxed, as though you were a very close observer, and just run through the sequence of events as they happened—as though you were doing no more than replaying a video. Some men imagine the inside of their forehead as a video screen.

2. Now start to pay special attention to what was happening around your body—inside and on the surface. Notice changes in body temperature, skin texture and perspiration, tensions, tremors, swellings, pulse/heart rate, visceral upset (for example, gut churning), etc.

Next notice all the things you were doing throughout the episode—with your words, voice, body movements, stance, etc.

Last, notice the range of emotional feelings and experiences, such as fear, hate, confusion, powerlessness, and so on, that occurred throughout the episode.

Pay a lot of attention to the change in signals, or their intensity, as you watch, hear, and feel yourself replaying the video from its low-level angry start to its full-blown raging conclusion.

3. When you are satisfied there is nothing left to see, hear, or feel, just let the video wind off to a blank screen, and become aware again of your breathing and your relaxed

state. Stay for a moment and recover your peace. Then lift yourself back up into the room, breathing steadily and more fully now. When you are ready, open your eyes.

4. Right away, pick up your pen or pencil and start writing down all of the things your body did, you did, and your emotions did or felt during the anger episode you just finished replaying. Let me repeat, leave nothing out; they are all useful and important as signals to your anger.

Feel free to talk to yourself—nobody will hear you! Interview yourself about the anger episode the way I interviewed Rajid on pages 156–158. If it helps, it's not crazy; if it doesn't help, don't do the interview. It doesn't matter *how* you do this task, just as long as you do it.

Just write as though your whole future depended upon it. Well, it does, doesn't it?

You cannot write too much for this exercise, but you can miss something important if you try to skip things. You will leave out vital signals if you try to sort things into relevant signals, and dismiss others as irrelevant, while you write. Much better to include everything that comes up, no matter what. You can sort it all out in step e.

5. When you have written down everything you can recall, go over your notes and extract from them everything that looks as if it might be a signal to your anger. Go back to my conversation with Rajid and see how I extracted and listed his signals afterwards in the table titled "Rajid's Anger Signals." Then, using the blank form titled "My Anger Signals," below, write all of your anger signals in the appropriate columns. Skip the "anger level" columns for now.

Note: If you have trouble relaxing yourself, recalling your last serious anger episode, or working through it to identify your physical, behavioral, and emotional signals, get someone to take you through this exercise by reading the above material aloud, starting with "Here's How to Relax." The content might feel unusual, but the practice of relaxation and guided exploration is widely used by counselors and psychotherapists everywhere.

That's it! You've identified your anger signals. In Chapter 11, we'll put them to work.

my anger signals

physical (around the body)	anger level	behavioral (actions and words)	anger level	emotional (feelings)	anger level

using your anger signals

In a dark wood I saw—I saw my several selves
Come running from the leaves,
Lewd, tiny, careless lives
That scuttled under stones,
Or broke, but would not go.

— *Theodore Roethke*[1]

By now, you should have three lists of your
anger signals: a list of your physical signals, a list of your
behavioral signals, and a list of your emotional signals. Of
course, in real-life anger episodes, these signals don't occur
in nice, neat lists. So now we need to reformat the lists so
that you can recognize your signals as they occur, and so that
they support your strategic choices, which we will address in
Chapter 12.

what happens when you get angry

When you replayed your last serious anger episode,
you might have noticed that you experienced quite different
signals as your anger level rose. You might also have noticed
that some signals kept on happening, but became faster or
more intense. Let's have a look at what happens for a number
of men when they get angry.

your signals change as your anger rises

I was handling it, you know? I mean I was sweating, and I know I was shouting, and I hated her. But I was in control . . . I thought. But then I could *feel* myself getting worse. I started banging the coffee table, and shoving things around on the top, and I just knew I was going to blow. Not long after that, I picked up the coffee table and threw it—just hurled it at the window. Jesus! What a bloody mess. God, I don't want to be like that!   (Fabian)

As your anger gets worse in any one episode, you might notice that new and different signals start to occur. For example, just when you start getting angry, you might be aware of a general body tension. You might start snapping your fingers or talking in a clipped, tight voice. Or, you might start feeling a little nervous and anxious. Just before you lose control, however, your heart may be pumping wildly, you might be punching the palm of one hand, and you might be feeling total hatred.

At higher levels of anger, you might experience quite different signals from those that were happening lower down your anger scale.

same signals—just bigger and faster!

As I replayed the episode, I noticed how I would be drumming my fingers on the edge of the table when we started arguing. But when I got really angry, I was banging away at 100 miles an hour.   (Darrol)

You might have some signals that just stay with you but get faster, more intense, or "heavier." Let's say one of your physical low-level anger signals is to perspire moderately; it may be that at higher levels of anger, you sweat profusely and saturate your clothes. Or, as you start to get angry, one of your behaviors might be to pace back and forth slowly with measured strides; when you are raging, you might pace rapidly, all around the room.

Emotional signals sometimes work in reverse. A common example is fear—at lower levels you might be quite scared of the situation you are in, of the people involved, or of one person or a likely event (e.g., getting badly hurt). But as your anger goes through the roof, you might notice that your fear has faded to nothing.[2]

> At first, I was so scared her brothers and their friends would pull me away and beat me up. But she just egged me on, you know? Just goaded and goaded about how she flirted and teased and could have had one of my own friends! I just blew it then. I didn't care what they did—they could all go and get fucked, for all I cared. They didn't worry me anymore; and I felt this weird calm feeling as I closed my fingers around her throat and... [crying now] ... Thank God they did pull me off!!   (Denver)

After the task from the previous chapter, it won't be too difficult for you to identify the different anger signals in the extracts from the stories of Fabian, Darrol, and Denver. But there's not much point in merely recognizing our anger signals if we can't make use of them.

the purpose of anger signals

There is only one purpose to be served by recognizing and recording our anger signals, and it is this: to be able to predict and control our rising anger.

Once you know the pattern in which your anger signals occur or intensify, then you can predict your own pattern of rising anger by the occurrence of those signals. Thus, when your level-one anger signals start to occur (physical, behavioral, and emotional), you know which signals to expect next. Then you can predict accurately what level of anger you will experience next. And so on up the scale. Now you can make a strategic choice: You can continue upwards until you lose control and do harm or damage, or you can take some other course of action to prevent or divert your anger. You might, for example, use one of the basic tools from Chapter 7, or an anger-release option from Chapter 8. (We will discuss strategic choices more fully in the next chapter.)

To make the best use of the anger signals you identified and recorded in the last chapter, we first have to re-sort them into an order that enables you to predict your own anger levels. We are going to convert them into progressive anger signals.

progressive anger signals

We need to reshuffle your anger signals, out of their present categories (physical, behavioral, and emotional) and into the order in which they actually occur as your anger rises.

You might be asking, "Why go through the exercise twice? Why take me through that difficult exercise of identifying my anger signals by type, and then turn around and take me through it again to identify their order?"

I agree that is a really good question, and not an easy one to answer. Let me put it this way—it's a bit like building one of those plastic models from a kit.

lachlan's strategy

I have a stepson who is crazy about building models—sometimes naval ships, mostly combat aircraft. You can't get past his bedroom door without stepping headfirst into the Battle of Britain! Lachlan is really good at building models these days. He has developed great skill and accuracy. But I still remember the first ones he put together. Here was this jumble of plastic bits and pieces (all gray of course), and there was this set of plans with numbers, symbols, elevations, cross-sections, under- and overviews everywhere.

The first thing Lachlan noticed was the very specific instructions about what order everything went together in. On paper, the different parts that went with their identifying number, and the sequence of construction, seemed quite straightforward. The problem was that he couldn't easily tell the difference between all the bits in their jumble of mountings. Worse, only the biggest and most obvious (such as wing and fuselage halves) seemed to look anything like their sketched representations on the plan.

But Lachlan is a fast learner and soon got the hang of things. The first thing he learned was that the construction task became much easier when he stopped trying to follow the plan, identify parts, and construct all at the same time. Now he has developed this order of tasks:

1. He examines the color picture of the finished aircraft or ship on the box.

2. Then, he glances at the plans and gets an overall impression of the major components and their spatial relationship to the whole.

3. Next, he gives some time and attention to each of the parts.

4. Then, he identifies each part with its function and location on the plans.

5. Only when he knows what the parts all look and feel like does he study the numbered order in which they are supposed to go together.

Lachlan's strategy for building models is smart because he learns to recognize the parts of the model before he learns their order of construction.

Most men are not as familiar with the process of exploring their anger as Lachlan is with the process of building models. The smart strategy for anger control is this: First learn to recognize your signals, then learn to recognize the levels they occur in. That's why we identified the anger signals in Chapter 10, and why we're dealing with progressive anger signals here. The difference is important.

As with model building, so with anger control; you need to have some sense of order, of sequence. That is about where the similarity ends. With model building, you need a vision or mental image of the finished product to guide and motivate your work. With anger control, you need a vision or mental image of flow and acceleration, of how your anger builds from its lower levels up to its peak of uncontrolled rage.

anger: does it come from outside or inside?

The only way to be able to recognize your different levels of rising anger is to know which of your anger signals occur or intensify at what anger levels. For some men, it is like a sudden explosion triggered by a minor event, after a slowly deepening but outwardly disguised bad mood:

> People would give me shit; it'd just be one of those days when things got worse and worse. But I'd smile and hold it in—bottle it all up, you know? Like the other day, after that awful family day thing, I got home and Angie was just leaving to go shopping with the baby. As soon as she backed out of the driveway, I started. Just blew up! Smashed the screen door and the front door. Threw stuff around inside...I don't know...coffee tables and knick-knacks and things like that. It was like a bloody hand grenade went off!
>
> (Josh)

For other men, it is like a storm thundering away aggressively all day:

> My wife says she just grabs the kids and takes off when I get like that. Even my dog hides under the bench in the shed when I start up. Everyone just gets out of my way. Maybe the mower won't start, maybe I'm out of gas, maybe the kids gave me shit. Who knows? But when I start throwing things, cursing and yelling, threatening people, and stomping around...I don't know, it must be pretty

bloody awful! And it just seems to go on and on—all day sometimes. (Peter)

Notice how Josh and Peter both experienced their anger as though it were something that happened *to* them, instead of something that happened *in* them. Notice also how little either of them seemed to know about what was happening. They could describe general mood and events *outside* of themselves, but they were unable yet to detail their progress through rising anger levels or experiences *inside* themselves. Not only were they unaware of their internal experiences (that is, they recognized no information or signals about their anger), they had no idea of the order of flow and acceleration. For Josh and Peter, that's all changed now.

Experiencing anger as something that happens *to* them is very common with the men who come to me for help. That is where the whole sense of losing control seems to come from. It seems logical, doesn't it? If it is something happening *to* me, then it is reasonable that I might not be able to control it. But if it is something happening *in* me, then I should be able to control it, right? Therefore, it must be something that is happening *to* me . . . perfect logic!

But the "logic" doesn't help, does it, because the worst thing that can happen *to* a man is to have control (over what is happening to him) taken away from him. In reality, of course, the only one who is taking control away is you; you surrender control. What's even worse, though, is that you don't feel there is anything you can do about it. So the cycle of anger goes around and gets deeper. Well, that is all about to change for you, too. But before you can use your anger signals to predict and control your rising anger, it helps to understand a few strategic features of rising anger levels.

anger levels

Anger levels can progress from mild annoyance right through to homicidal rage.

Remember that in Chapter 3, we talked about how our experience of anger can range from the trivial to the terrifying. At the lowest levels is the annoyance of some interruption to our daily routine. At the highest extreme is the terrible rage that seemed to have driven that Tasmanian cabinetmaker to slaughter his children and himself. I guess that many of us would like to say that since our anger is "normal," no worse than the lowest level, we are really only reading this book to keep our partners happy. Most of us would also be saying that there is no chance of us ever going as far as that disturbed cabinetmaker. We are just not that violent, right?

Wrong! The three key factors that seem to make the most difference to anger outcomes are these:

- Our level of anger arousal (how angry we are)
- Our level of awareness of the consequences of what we are doing
- Our perceived level of self-control

Sadly, our conscious awareness of consequences and our subjective level of self-control both seem to deteriorate as our anger levels rise.

Don't forget this: We are not talking about *violent strategy* or its planned (premeditated) potential for violent outcomes. We are talking about *violent anger* and its unplanned (spontaneous) potential for violent outcomes.

anger levels and the threshold of risk

In my experience with angry people, I have found it useful to work with four artificially divided levels of anger. This is no more than a strategic way for client and therapist to understand and respond effectively to the lower levels, the higher levels, and the threshold of risk in between.

The "threshold of risk" is an artificially designated zone between the two lower levels of anger and the two higher levels. It is illustrated by the traffic-light model for anger and risk, discussed in the next subsection. Once your anger rises past the threshold, you are at serious risk of losing control, and that is when you are most likely to do harm or damage. The objective must be to keep your anger level below the threshold of risk.

The notion of the threshold of risk is all about control. For any anger-control system to work, we need to maintain our awareness of consequences and our residual level of self-control, our ability to think about and control what we actually do. Therefore, we need some practical ways of knowing not so much *when* we are in control or out of control but rather *what happens* to our bodies, our behavior, and our emotions *up to and at the point where we lose control.* After that, it is all a bit too late! That is why recognizing our threshold of risk, and the warning signals supplied by our progressive anger signals, is so important.

Our progressive anger signals can play a vital part in preventing our anger from spiraling upwards. Not only do they tell us we are angry or are becoming angry, but with practice, they can tell us just how angry we are and how close we are to our threshold of risk. Like traffic lights, our signals can tell us when to stop—before it is too late.

traffic lights for anger levels and risk

The traffic-light model is universally understood by just about everyone in our society who ever uses a major road. The model works well as a metaphor for our anger levels, warning signals, and risk.

Every driver knows that a set of traffic lights means an intersection or some other road hazard at which, were it not for the lights, there would be a significant risk. Green, therefore, doesn't mean rocket through at top speed; it means approach with care and proceed only if the road is clear! Yellow doesn't mean plant your foot on the gas to make it through the

	traffic-light model for anger and risk
Level 1	*Green light—Approach with care.* Are you just starting to get angry; do you still care about consequences; are you determined to keep self-control?
Level 2	*Yellow light—Prepare to stop.* Are you feeling really angry—approaching your threshold but able to make strategic choices? **threshold of risk**
Level 3	*Red light—STOP NOW.* Have you gone past your threshold; are you about to lose control, but still able to pull back or escape?
Level 4	*You've gone through a red light—get off the road!* Have you lost care and control?

intersection before the red light; it means slow down and prepare to stop—you are at high risk of doing harm and damage if you proceed. And red, of course, unequivocally means STOP NOW. Ignore a red light and, unless you are unbelievably lucky, you will cause damage, serious injury, or death.

Using the traffic-light model, here is one way to picture your threshold of risk. Close your eyes and imagine you are behind the wheel of your car. You are sitting at the traffic lights, about to drive into the busiest and most awesome intersection you have ever seen. Across your side of the road is painted a very wide white strip, behind which you have stopped. Unless you have the green light, you are at the mercy of the deadliest traffic in the world once you cross that white strip. That is your threshold of risk—cross it at your peril!

making anger signals progressive

In face-to-face work, converting a man's anger signals to progressive anger signals is an easy task. In one session, we can identify his anger signals. In our next session, I ask him to recall his last serious anger episode briefly, and then I hand him a printed copy of his anger signals. Next, I draw the traffic-light model on my whiteboard and call out his signals one by one. I ask him to rank his anger, on a scale of one to four, when that signal occurred. On another sheet of paper, I regroup the signals into those four levels and give my client a copy. That becomes his log of progressive anger signals.

other men's progressive anger signals

To get a better idea of the process, look at the listing of Fabian's, Kevin's, and Michael's anger signals that appear on pages 187–189.

Notice how this time a column headed "anger levels" is inserted alongside the columns for each of the three types of signals; in that column the three men have recorded a score of 1 to 4 beside each signal. The score indicates the anger level in which that particular signal occurs or intensifies. Notice how some higher-level signals are intensified versions of lower-level signals (e.g., increased tension, palms sweat more).

now it's your turn

Create your own progressive anger signals by following these steps:

1. Read through "Anger Levels," immediately below, and have it in front of you while you work.

   Anger Levels

   Level 1: I'm starting to get angry—but still care about the consequences.

   Level 2: I'm feeling really angry—approaching my threshold.

My Threshold of Risk

Level 3: I've gone past my threshold—but could still pull back and control it.

Level 4: I've lost it completely.

2. Recall your last serious anger episode.

3. Now go through all the anger signals you recorded in the chart titled "My Anger Signals," on page 174. As you work through your signals, assign them a score of 1, 2, 3, or 4, according to the level of anger you experienced. The number you assign should be your *best guess* as to what level of anger you have reached when that particular signal occurs or intensifies.

tips for this task

- As you review each of your signals, try to *re-feel*—rather than *re-think*—what it's like when those signals happen. That way you will be able to recall more clearly, through your bodily and emotional sensations, how angry you were at the time.

- I know this is a practical task in which you were urged to use your head, but when you assign an anger level (1 to 4) to each signal, go with what seems to fit best at gut level, rather than with what you *think* should be right at head level. If you do this, you will guarantee getting it right.

- When you have assigned a score to each signal, you have completed the conversion of your anger signals to progressive anger signals. Use them frequently. Whenever you can make some time, relax and review a serious anger episode; if not the last one, the one before that, and then the one before that again.

- Until it comes as second nature, always do your anger-episode reviews the way we've done them in this book.

fabian

physical (around the body)	anger level	behavioral (actions and words)	anger level	emotional (feelings)	anger level
Abdominal heat erupting	4	Doing uncontrolled and vicious things	4	Anger erupting like a volcano	4
Heat brewing in stomach	3		3	Fear (of men) is fading out	3
Energy rush developing	3	"Don't hit women rule" clicks on			
Previous cues going numb	3		1		
	2	Speech becoming tightly controlled			
Eyes watering	2				
Muscles tightening	2				
Lips drying	2				
Slight body shaking	1				
Slight general tension developing					

First, do the Chapter 10 tasks of deep relaxation and signal identification. Then, on another day, do the Chapter 11 task of converting them to progressive anger signals. Repeat this if you were uncertain of the score (1 to 4) to assign to your signals the first time around.

kevin

physical (around the body)	anger level	behavioral (actions and words)	anger level	emotional (feelings)	anger level
Frothing at the mouth	4	Voice rising	1	Guts "tied in knots"	3
Voice quivering	1	Yelling	2	Feeling upset	3
Quivering and shaking	2	Standing "nose-to-nose"	3	Feeling driven to smash opponent in the mouth	4
Getting tense	2	Standing up	2		
Getting hot	3	Closing/opening fists	3	Feeling hated by the world	3
	3	Bracing legs	3		
Sweat dripping off brow	3	Screaming	3		
Body tensing more	3	Striking	4		
Hair on neck standing up		Pacing and moving	2		
		Smashing walls or car	4		

- The more often you do these tasks, the more you will know about your anger, and the more you will be able to predict and control it.

- Ranking your anger signals progressively is an essential step if you're going to make them work *for* you, instead of *against* you and those around you. Still, you might find it difficult working alone to reformat them into the order in which they occur as your anger rises. As always, if you find

michael

physical (around the body)	anger level	behavioral (actions and words)	anger level	emotional (feelings)	anger level
Heart beating faster and louder	1	Yelling and screaming	3	Feeling urge to break something	3
Breath getting short	1	Balling fists	4		
Head and ears start getting hot	1	Breaking something or hitting someone with fist, hand, or object	4		
Shoulders and chest getting tight	2				
Getting hotter	2				
	3				
Arms and hands shaking					
	3				
Tension and tightness Increasing					

you cannot do it alone, get help from a counselor or someone else who you think is willing and able to help you complete this important task.

– Once you have reformatted your anger signals, they can alert you to your rising anger next time it happens. Now let us turn to the main objective of PAM (personal anger monitor): to enable you to make the best strategic choices when you actually find yourself getting angry.

making strategic choices

Whether you think you can or whether you think you can't, you are right.

— Henry Ford[1]

There is an old axiom that says, "Knowledge is power."

If you know how your anger works—its sources, its triggers, its levels, and its thresholds of risk—you have the power to control it. At this stage in working through this book, you now know much more about your anger than you have ever known. Armed with your basic tools for preventing anger, your anger release options, and your progressive anger signals, you also have all the information and resources you need to control your anger. All you now need is the will to make and execute one of four strategic choices, which will vary only with your level of anger.

You do not need to *think rationally* about these choices when you are *feeling emotionally* angry, because there is only one strategic choice to make at each level of anger.[2] This is where the work you did on your progressive anger signals really pays off. All those signals can be recognized and responded to from within the emotional experience of your anger. You just need to become as familiar with them as you can—consciously!

Yes, knowledge is indeed power!

And knowledge of yourself and your anger signals is power over yourself . . . and over your anger.

anger levels and strategic choices

There is a single objective to which all of Part III so far has been leading: to give you the spontaneous ability to make *one strategic choice* when you are angry—at whatever level. For all practical purposes, this whole system for controlling anger—your personal anger monitor—rides or falls on your ability to make strategic choices for action at any of the four different levels of anger. The single mission of this system is not just to recognize your anger signals and at what level they occur, but to keep you at anger levels *you can control*. One by one, let's spell out what is meant by each strategic choice. Here are your four strategic choices:

level 1: prevent or express your anger

At anger level 1, you can choose between preventing your anger from emerging at all or expressing your anger as it is.

Now, I realize a lot of people, especially my professional peers, are going to jump in here and protest. "That's no choice at all; anger should be expressed," they'll say, "appropriately, rationally, calmly, and without intimidation or threat to the other person involved." And I agree—of course people should express their anger. But there are times, places, and circumstances—*for those who are struggling right now with a serious anger problem*—where this may not be a good idea. What I am saying is that you have a choice. Use that choice!

For people who have a serious problem with their anger—in that it gets out of control and they do harm or damage—the *safest* strategic alternative *for now* is to prevent anger from rising. You can always *return* to express your anger when you've thought about it, when you feel safer and more confident in your ability to control it.

how to prevent your anger from rising

1. Make sure it is *anger* you're feeling! Take three deep breaths, and check out your progressive anger signals for level 1 anger. If it's not anger, tell yourself what it is, and find the courage to own it. Many men are so out of touch with their pain and fear that they think they are angry when really they are hurt or scared. Or, maybe you're sure it's anger— but the anger is actually *hiding* some other emotion that makes you feel more vulnerable, such as pain or fear. As we've learned, we men are often quick to get angry, in order to shield us from feeling those other, "nonmasculine," more vulnerable emotions. If this is the case, be courageous: Own up to them.

I was so bloody furious: The kid is only ten years old. He had no business climbing on the roof at all! When he slipped...well, it was just luck I was in the shed. I heard him yell. I just raced over and caught him as the gutter gave way. Jeez, did he get a lashing!   (Henry)

four strategic choices

At Anger Level 1	You can: Prevent your anger	Or: Express your anger
At Anger Level 2	You can: Divert and release your anger	Or: Allow your anger to rise
threshold of risk		
At Anger Level 3	You can: Divert and release your anger	Or: Allow your anger to rise
At Anger Level 4	You can: Escape	Or: Lose control

2. If it *is* anger—and you have chosen to prevent it from rising—use one of the basic tools for preventing anger, described in Chapter 7. Read that chapter frequently, each time searching your own life and routines for opportunities to create new and different versions of "The Off Button," "The Difference Maker," and "The Risk Taker."

how to express your anger effectively and appropriately

1. Be confident, not coercive.

   You need to feel confident you can control your anger at this level. This means knowing that you are as entitled to feel and express your anger as you are those other feelings that we have been discussing. But it does not mean you can use your anger to bully or coerce the other person into submission—that is not what this is about. On the contrary, when you express your anger confidently and assertively to people, they may well come to know that you feel angry at their words or actions as you heard and saw them, but they should not come to feel degraded, assaulted, victimized, or demonized as a person or forced into cowering submission. If they do feel any of those, it might be because you are behaving *coercively* instead of *confidently* in your expression of anger towards them. Feeling confident is your right and responsibility; being coercive is abusive behavior. Feeling confident also means knowing the right time, place, and relationship to express your anger. Which takes us to the second rule.

2. Be clear and focused.

   Direct your anger to whom or what it belongs. If you are angry at your colleague Tom, don't save it up to deliver to your wife Maria. Tell it to Tom—at the time, assertively and clearly. Similarly, if the lawnmower just blew up, yell at *it*, now—not at your son Bill or daughter Wendy half a day later.

3. Use an "I" statement, not a "you" statement.

Usually, when people are angry, they start with an accusation or a blaming statement about the other person. It's all over then—the only way to go from there is a fight. Try to start everything you say with an "I" statement. For anger, there is a rule of thumb that works almost every time; I call it the "*I feel angry when I . . .*" rule.

Simply put, when I'm feeling angry, I start by saying how I feel, absolutely *not* what you did or didn't do. *Never, never,* ever use that kind of blaming statement—the word "you" at the beginning of a sentence is a dead giveaway to a blaming statement—when you're angry. Always, *always, always* express your anger with a statement that starts this way: "I feel angry when I..." Here are some examples of "I" statements for when you're feeling angry:

- "I feel angry when I hear you say that."

- "I feel really pissed off when I see you driving my car without asking me first."

- "I feel hurt and angry when I come home to find you with another man."

Sticking to these kinds of statements guarantees that you will be fair, open, and accurate. No one can contest the fact that I feel something—in this case, anger—when I hear or see something. I might have *seen* or *heard* wrong, but I know what I *feel*, and that's inarguable.

The best part of the "I feel angry when I..." rule is that it never blames anyone for anything, whether they did something wrong or not. It just declares how you feel. The business of sorting out whether someone is to blame, or is to be held responsible for something, belongs to the head's intelligence, not to the heart's emotion.

The "I feel angry when I..." rule is the best-known communication tool for expressing anger safely and well.

Finally, as I said earlier, this system is not an interpersonal communication tool. Please go shopping for a good communication program. It will help you express yourself more effectively, and it might also help your family.

level 2: divert and release your anger

It is most important to pay close attention to your progressive anger signals for level 2, and to work to become clear about the differences between level 2 signals and level 3 signals. At level 2, you are in serious anger territory; your threshold of risk is approaching, and it is really easy to slip over it—as you well know. It is much safer and more effective to make a choice to divert and release your anger at this level than it is once you're over the threshold and into level 3. Remember the power saw in Chapter 9? It is here, at level 2, that the "saw" is well into the cut but still able to be withdrawn. It is much harder to do that in level 3, where you really have to grope for the "power source" to unplug it, and it's so far away and hazy.

I didn't know what was happening. I mean, I *did* know, but things were starting to get jumbled up a bit. I was scared, in a way, to stay in the room with her. I knew she'd keep going at me, and I knew I couldn't take much more before I lashed out. Yet it was so hard to leave and, you know, back down, or something. Thank God I knew my signals and knew where I'd be next! So I bolted! I said I was going for a jog, and I'd be back in an hour to sort it out. And then I was off... running like crazy.

About an hour later, I came home, exhausted! But I had calmed right down by then. Rosemary wasn't stressed out or scared, not the way she used to be when we'd fight and I'd go over the top and lose it. So, yeah, we sorted it out okay. Not that it happens often these days. Jesus, I can't remember the last time something like that happened.

(Kevin)

Kevin acted safely; he avoided passing his threshold of risk. Not only did he calm down, but his wife felt safer and less stressed.

how to divert and release your anger

1. You don't really divert your anger at this point; you divert yourself! You declare that you are getting very angry and that you are going to leave, cool down, and come back later to resolve the issue.

Yes, you can do this when it's an object you're mad at; just try not to get caught!

I was getting bloody mad at the chainsaw; it just wouldn't start no matter what. I'd done everything—plug, mixture, carburetor, the lot. So I slammed it down on the bench and I yelled at it, "I'm going out and I'll be back to sort you out. So don't go away!"

Next thing this voice comes back at me with, "Yeah, right then. And would you like me to start myself and chew up your bench while you're gone?"

Course it was bloody Bruce from next door... we both cracked up. Just had to see the funny side, ha ha.   (Barry)

2. Choose an anger release option from the raft of AROs you built in Chapter 8.

Put all your anger energy into the ARO for as long as it takes to make you feel tired.

Return to the scene of your anger and/or the other person involved and attempt the second option in the strategic choice for level 1: "Express your anger." Reread the instructions for level 1, above, before you attempt this step.

how to allow your anger to rise

Do what you've always done until now, unless you really want your life, and the lives of those around you, to improve—in which case choose the first option!

level 3: divert and release your anger at a higher level of stress

The steps for level 3 are identical to those for level 2, but the degrees of difficulty and stress are much greater. I just can't emphasize enough the importance of making the strategic choice to divert and release your anger at level 2, where you are much more in control and less stressed than you will be at level 3. In terms of the traffic-light model (page 184), you are facing a red light at level 3, and you are very close to charging through it into a possibly deadly situation—deadly for you and for everyone around you. You can still back off, take a diversion, and go, immediately, to an anger release option from your raft of AROs. But it is going to take every last bit of control, determination, and strength that you have. Your "power saw" is now well and truly committed to the cut of conflict; violence (emotional or physical) is only a snarl away. There is harm or damage on the horizon. You can still withdraw, but you will have to pull the plug—NOW!

level 4: escape or lose control

Escaping anger—or, more specifically, escaping the scene and the other people in your angry episode—is a strategy that has special importance and value at the higher levels of anger. At level 4, you have gone way past your threshold and you are on the brink of losing control. You have one last choice: to just let it all go, or to escape.

Remember: At this point, it is still your choice whether you lose control—or escape.

how to escape your situation

The escape option requires no thinking, feeling, consideration of alternatives, or evaluation. It is simply a cut-and-run option that gets you (and your partner or other antagonist) out of the heat. Escape cuts off the immediate risk clean as a whistle. Your antagonist may be calling you with everything he knows, or goading you to turn back and fight, or deliberately insulting you. If your antagonist is angry at you or feels hurt by you, one certainty is that you will be hit with a barrage of provocative threats and expletives. These are not necessarily designed to test your resolve but to express your antagonist's anger and pain—stuff you know a lot about by now. Your single-minded task is to escape. Why? *Because the last thing you will want to discover later is that you have done harm or damage to your family or home.*

Escape means leave the scene, go outside, get away—ON FOOT!

- **DO NOT DRINK!** Alcohol lowers your threshold, raises the risks, and reduces your control.

- **DO NOT DRIVE!** Driving is deadly for the angry man and everyone else on the road.

- **DO NOT DRINK AND DRIVE!** Drunk and angry driving is the most fatal combination of all.

No matter what anyone says to you—no matter whether it is your wife, partner, kids, relatives, or friends—your single task, when you have gone this far beyond your threshold, is to escape. There is only one person or class of person in the world whom you should allow to dissuade you from your escape, and that's a police officer performing his or her duty.

Nobody in the world knows your threshold level as well as you. Nobody knows what the internal emotional experience of your anger is like, except you. Whatever anyone tells you, there is one fact both you and I know about you, and it is this: You, and you alone, are the best expert there is about *your* anger.[3] Therefore, once you choose the escape option, you have done so upon the best-available expert advice.

Your wife or partner might not like your taking off, especially in the middle of a big argument, even though your anger might scare her. But you know that your first responsibility is clear: that is, to guarantee the safety of the women and children around you. You should alert your family about what to expect when you get angry, but they still might forget. So you might have to explain again afterwards. So what? Better to go through it all again and again than to risk harm or damage even once, right? If you're still in doubt, talk it through with a counselor.

Okay, so you escaped. Now, as with the anger diversion strategy, once you've escaped, you need to release your anger energy quickly. Choose an ARO as soon as you are able, and give it all the energy you have.

caution

Anger release options that require any material, tools, or equipment are extremely dangerous for you and anyone else while you are still at anger level 4.

Yes, knowledge is power, and you now have a lot of power over your anger. Next, we'll display that knowledge, so you can check out PAM, your personal anger monitor, at a single glance.

your personal anger monitor

O! Let me not be mad, not mad, sweet heaven;
Keep me in temper; I would not be mad!

— *William Shakespeare*[1]

Welcome to PAM, a personal anger monitor designed to be a valuable and practical partner for you. PAM displays on paper everything you now know about your anger, how a serious anger episode usually proceeds, and what you need to do in the future to control it. PAM includes your progressive anger signals and levels, your strategic choices, and the tools you need to execute them when you are angry. In short, PAM's task is to help you control your anger.

So who or what *is* this PAM?

pam[2]

PAM is not always attractive, does not have a great figure, never massages your ego, and won't hang onto your arm and smile seductively at you in public just so you feel good. In fact, PAM takes no bullshit from you or anyone else; PAM's eyes and ears miss nothing about you or about what is really going on inside you.

PAM is one of the world's greatest straight shooters: calls a spade a spade, can read you like a book, and sticks by you through thick and thin...as long as you ask. PAM could be your best friend.

When you start getting hot under the collar and the heat gets turned up around you, having PAM with you is like having your own personal firefighter. When you get angry, PAM asks only one thing of you:

When PAM starts talking, you start listening.

PAM is your personal anger monitor.

PAM's objective is to keep you from doing harm or damage when you get angry.

how pam works

At lower, subthreshold anger levels, PAM alerts you to your current level of anger, how close you are to your threshold of risk, and when you can expect to lose control.

At higher, superthreshold anger levels, PAM reminds you of the risks your anger poses to yourself, other people, and/or property.

By alerting you to your current level of anger and control, PAM prompts you to other, different choices about actions you can take to prevent your anger from rising further, to divert your anger into an anger release option, or to escape altogether.

pam's features for anger control

Your personal anger monitor appears on page 209. Notice it is not yet complete, because the boxes on the left are still empty. Fabian's, Kevin's, and Michael's PAMs appear on pages 203–205 and have been completed. Notice that the boxes on the left contain their progressive anger signals at their relevant anger levels. Your own progressive anger signals are the important features needed to complete your PAM.

If you are still uncertain about your anger signals and how they get converted into progressive anger signals, please go back and reread Chapters 10 and 11. Those signals, when you experience them, tell you how angry you are—your anger level.

There are four levels, separated by your threshold of risk, as we discussed previously. Your anger levels, 1–4, are designated in your PAM in the slim columns to the right of where you will copy your anger signals a little later. If you are unsure about your anger levels, please review Chapter 11.

To the right of each designated anger level are your strategic choices. These are universal and remain fixed, regardless of the huge differences in anger signals between men. There is in practice only one choice between two options at each level of anger. Therefore, you have nothing to think about at any level beyond level 1. Once you've gone past level 1, all you have to do at any anger level is recognize your signals and respond with a single choice.

Recognize and respond—that's it!

If you are not quite clear about strategic choices, read Chapter 12 again.

In the far right-hand column are your tools. These, too, are arranged to match your strategic choices and their corresponding anger levels. We discussed your basic tools in Chapter 7, and you built your raft of AROs in Chapter 8. You can develop your own anger-prevention tools to suit your life, routines, and anger triggers. Your raft of AROs can be expanded or modified to suit your health, fitness, environment, and resources. Please review your tools and AROs frequently and practice them— even (or especially) in nonangry moods.

other men's pams

Take your time and thoroughly read the personal anger monitors of Fabian, Kevin, and Michael in the pages that follow. Pay special attention to the way they have transferred their

fabian's pam

progressive anger signals	anger level	strategic choice	tools
* I have slight general tension. * My speech is controlled.	1	Prevent your anger. or Express your anger.	Use Anger Avoidance Toolkit. Use rule: "I feel angry when I . . . "
* My eyes water. * My muscles tighten. * My lips are dry. * My body is shaking slightly.	2	Divert and release your anger. or Allow it to rise.	Declare your anger. Excuse yourself and leave. Choose an ARO. Return within stated time.

threshold of risk

progressive anger signals	anger level	strategic choice	tools
* Heat brews in my stomach. * An energy rush develops. * My fear (of men) is fading out. * Physically, I am numb. * My "don't hit women rule" clicks in.	3	Divert and release your anger. or Allow it to rise.	Declare your anger. Excuse yourself and leave. Choose an ARO. Return within stated time.
* My internal heat and anger erupt. * My behavior is uncontrolled and vicious.	4	ESCAPE! or Lose control.	GO!—NOW! Don't drink or drive. When anger has eased, choose an ARO.

kevin's pam

progressive anger signals	anger level	strategic choice	tools
* My voice quivers. * My voice starts to rise * My body starts to get tense. * I feel my mood changing.	1	Prevent your anger. or Express your anger.	Use Anger Avoidance Toolkit. Use rule: "I feel angry when I . . ."
* My body quivers and shakes. * I'm getting much more tense. * I'm getting hot. * I'm standing up (if not already). * I'm pacing and moving around. * I'm yelling.	2	Divert and release your anger. or Allow it to rise.	Declare your anger. Excuse yourself and leave. Choose an ARO. Return within stated time.

threshold of risk

* Sweat is dripping off my brow. * My body is tense. * Hair on my neck is standing up. * I'm standing "nose-to-nose." * My fists are closing and opening. * My legs are braced. * I'm yelling and screaming. * My gut's feeling tied in a knot. * I'm feeling upset. * I'm feeling like the world hates me.	3	Divert and release your anger. or Allow it to rise.	Declare your anger. Excuse yourself and leave. Choose an ARO. Return within stated time.
* I'm frothing at the mouth. * I'm hitting someone. * I'm smashing walls or car. * I'm feeling driven to smash opponent in the mouth.	4	ESCAPE! or Lose control.	GO!—NOW! Don't drink or drive. When anger has eased, choose an ARO.

michael's pam

progressive anger signals	anger level	strategic choice	tools
* My head and ears start to get hot. * My breathing get short. * My heart beats faster and louder.	1	Prevent your anger. or Express your anger.	Use Anger Avoidance Toolkit. Use rule: "I feel angry when I . . ."
* My arms and hands shake. * I am getting hotter. * My shoulders and chest get tight.	2	Divert and release your anger. or Allow it to rise.	Declare your anger. Excuse yourself and leave. Choose an ARO. Return within stated time.

threshold of risk

* I feel the urge to break something. * I am yelling and screaming. * My tension and tightness goes up.	3	Divert and release your anger. or Allow it to rise.	Declare your anger. Excuse yourself and leave. Choose an ARO. Return within stated time.
* I am smashing something or someone * My fists are bunched and I'm fighting.	4	ESCAPE! or Lose control.	GO!—NOW! Don't drink or drive. When anger has eased, choose an ARO.

progressive anger signals from the forms in Chapter 11, and entered them on their PAMs in the far left-hand column, corresponding to the appropriate anger level. To remind yourself of the process, have another look at the original lists of their anger signals on pages 165–168 in Chapter 10. Remember, also, the process you went through to convert your own anger signals to *progressive* anger signals in Chapter 11.

Notice the differences and similarities between these three men's progressive anger signals. No matter whether you found you had very different signals, or signals very similar to any of theirs, you are a normal angry man. It really is neither significant nor important whether your anger signals seem to you outrageous or trivial. What matters is that they are reliable indicators of your anger at different levels.

It also matters that you own them. By that, I mean you should try to see your anger signals as parts of yourself. Anything you can do to bring responsibility and ownership of your anger back to yourself is helpful and important. If you blame others for making you angry, you give away your own power and control over yourself to someone else.

One good way to own your anger signals is to express them as action (verb) phrases, instead of just naming them.

For example, compare these two anger signals: "Loud yells and screams" versus "I am yelling and screaming."

And what about these? "There is a general tension" versus "My body winds up all over—like a spring!"

Another strong way to own your signals is to express them in "I" or "my" statements. Notice in the examples above that one of each pair owns the signal, whereas the other keeps a certain distance, almost as if it is happening "out there" instead of "in here."

When you read Fabian's, Kevin's, and Michael's PAMs, see how they have used action phrases and "I" or "my" statements as often as possible. Most of their signals do this; some don't. They are real men, after all!

your pam

Now it is your turn to complete your own personal anger monitor. Take your time and follow the steps.

the steps for completing your pam

1. On page 209, you will find a form titled "My Personal Anger Monitor." For your personal use, you are welcome to reproduce this form on a copier or computer before you fill it in. That way, you can update or renew your PAM as often as you need to, if and when your anger signals change.

2. Now turn back to your log of progressive anger signals at the end of Chapter 10, on page 174. Copy each anger signal onto your personal anger monitor, into the empty box to the left of the corresponding anger level. If you need help, study the examples of Fabian, Kevin, and Michael.

3. As you complete your PAM, practice "listening" to your body, "replaying" your behaviors, and feeling your emotions; do this not only when you're feeling angry, but in all of your emotional states—including joy and excitement. (More about this below.)

4. PAM is most important. Get help if you can't do it alone.

You will see by now that PAM is the most important gauge you can have for your anger. If you want to control your anger and guarantee safety for your family, you have to be able to learn and read your PAM. So it has to be right. As with all of the previous steps you've taken while working through this book, go for professional help if you find you can't do this on your own. Take this book along and ask the therapist or counselor to work through the anger-control system with you and to help you to build your PAM.

listening to your body

You will find that "listening" to your body actually does improve your awareness of all your different emotions. For example, when you find yourself fighting back tears, you know you are sad, hurt, or grieving somehow. As we saw in Part II, it is important to express those feelings, either at the time or as soon as it is practical and safe. (But consider—if you are a pilot, during your landing approach is not the most practical time to express your grief!)

As you practice, you really can use your body to help you distinguish between your emotions. Your anger signals will become distinct and obvious to you as soon as they start.

maintaining pam for anger control

Using PAM well is not too different from using any set of gauges or instruments. It takes information, skill, practice, and an ear for variance, an eye for change. Take your car, for example, or a diesel-driven pump. You know when it's under load by the change in sounds. If there's a cylinder out, you not only hear the sound shift, you see the engine rocking more on its mounts. At least, you *can* do those things *if you know* what you're looking and listening for. The only way to get those skills is to learn and practice. If you're willing to do that for your car or your stereo system or any other equipment, what about doing it for you?

We started all this head stuff in the shed—with my angry power saw. We went through basic tools and AROs, and we have pretty well wrapped up PAM. Now you have a complete anger-control system to practice and use. That brings us back to the shed and to the stool you are sitting on—and a couple of empty mugs. Well, I don't know about you, but I'm tired! So I'm off for a fresh cup of coffee.

Oh! Speaking of engines and fuel and all, we're going to take a look at the energy of anger next and then some ideas for putting it to good use.

Now, that would be different, wouldn't it?

my personal anger monitor

progressive anger signals	anger level	strategic choice	tools
	1	Prevent your anger. or Express your anger.	Use Anger Avoidance Toolkit. Use rule: "I feel angry when I . . ."
	2	Divert and release your anger. or Allow it to rise.	Declare your anger. Excuse yourself and leave. Choose an ARO (page 147). Return within stated time.

threshold of risk

	3	Divert and release your anger. or Allow it to rise.	Declare your anger. Excuse yourself and leave. Choose an ARO (page 147). Return within stated time.
	4	ESCAPE! or Lose control.	GO!—NOW! Don't drink or drive. When anger has eased, choose an ARO (page 147).

part four

...now with
your energy!

anger and energy

If you have a rage in you, you can manifest the energy.
You can tame it. You can give it purpose.

— *Angry Anderson*[1]

Back in Chapter 2, anger was described as an intense emotional experience through which we express our fear and pain. Throughout this book, I have tried to show how some of the taken-for-granted, but no less painful, experiences of our childhood, adolescence, and early adulthood might have a major influence upon our emotional development and health later on. Steve Biddulph describes these experiences as the "wounds of childhood," which in later life, if unhealed, "can leave you either paralyzed and depressed...or...can make you grandiose and over-achieving."[2] That suppressed pain, in other words, will gain expression through emotional or even physical manifestations.

the energy of anger[3]

Biddulph's work is an elegant expression of emotional pain—however old and long-held—as energy. Like all energy forms, one way or another, sooner or later, that energy will seek expression or release. For men, the most common expression of emotional or physical pain is anger.

In both extreme and routine ways, masculine development through childhood, adolescence, and young manhood often becomes riddled with the seeds and sanctions of failure. In our struggle to measure up and survive as men, we seem to cut off all those other, more emotional parts of ourselves that might get in the way of our central purpose—to be real men.

What we *actually* learn is to cut ourselves off from our emotional parts, to suppress our emotions. The truth is that all those emotional experiences continue for us, whether we like it or not. By attempting to suppress our emotions, we simply set up an internal program diverting all of our negative emotional energy into anger.

The problem with so many of the rules for manhood is that they seem to run afoul of as many laws of nature.

energy in equals energy out

Think about all the negative emotional energy stored up inside your average young man by the time he's twenty-one—expressed mostly as anger. In the last three years, several doctors have asked me what they can do about angry young men: what programs they can refer them to and how they can get them to come in to discuss the problem. Oh yes, it is always their girlfriends, sisters, mothers, and later their wives who visit physicians and social service agencies for help with their young men's anger.

Think about *how* all that energy comes out so often as anger.

Sure, anger is indeed intense emotional experience. Anger is also the expression of intense internal energy—the accumulation of a lifetime of unexpressed pain, fear, and sadness. And anger will come out . . . one way or another.

Be honest now. At the same time as you have felt that intense emotional experience of anger, have you not also felt an intense surge of energy?

Isn't anger energizing? Anger *is* energy.

The problem is that, like any internal experience of surging energy, anger energy can be very seductive, even intoxicating.

Fabian (whom you've met in several chapters of this book) had a lot of trouble resisting the seductive intoxication of his anger. Working as a hotel bouncer, he would reach a point in his management of a difficult customer where he would start getting angry. Seduced by the buzz, Fabian would invite the customer to respond with violent or threatening behavior, so that Fabian experienced himself being seduced into abandoning control and thus allowing his anger to flourish into full fury.

But there is an upside to anger: You actually can divert the energy of anger towards producing something positive for yourself and for others. How many times in your life have you seen anger fuel the determination needed to complete a particularly frustrating but positive task? My own anger drives my struggle to succeed! The irony is that when I engage that struggle with positive determination and courage, I begin to grow as a person.

finding positive energy from anger

Terry (whom you met in Chapter 3), a crusader for his church's campaign against an application to open a brothel in a large regional center in rural Australia, also experienced the seductive power of his anger energy (some Australian states operate what is known as a "containment policy," whereby prostitution either has been legalized or decriminalized but must be relegated to medically supervised, regulated, and policed premises). Usually a silent supporter in public, Terry found himself the only church member willing to get up and actually speak against the proposal in a crowded public hearing. Terry discovered the allure of that energy burst, tempered by the goal he had focused on. For the first time in his life, Terry found himself both heard and listened to. Who knows what contribution Terry made to the decision of the brothel applicants to withdraw their application and resubmit later for another location?

The point here is that Terry belonged to a community of interest whose views he shared, and he became able to advance those views publicly—by using his anger in a goal-focused way.

Previously, Terry's anger energy was expressed—after long periods of internalization—in emotionally and verbally abusive conflict with his wife over longstanding issues between them that kept bringing the painful abuses of his childhood back to the surface. Prior to psychotherapy, Terry's personality had disintegrated into (at least) three "parts"—a presentation often labeled "multiple personality disorder." The antibrothel campaign occurred during his period of therapy with me. After his involvement in the campaign, Terry's progress towards reintegration into one person accelerated as he became able to deal with the pain and fear that drove his anger. At the conclusion of therapy, Terry was a "new man."

This energy paradigm pervades much of the work I do with clients struggling to deal with their anger. First, we recognize and accept anger as a normal and valid human experience; then, we encourage creative, practical, and positive ways of expressing and releasing anger energy. Some of these you were introduced to as anger release options in Part III. Now let us consider how you can actually use these AROs and other, more surprising pursuits for converting large amounts of your anger into worthwhile and beneficial outcomes.

energy: the fire of anger

Because anger has become seen as the least acceptable, and the most feared, of the so-called negative emotions in this age of rationalism, we have become disabled from recognizing anger as an emotional energy force common to human nature. As with all things in nature, there are two ways of dealing with energy—you can work *against* it or you can work *with* it. Working against nature is usually expensive, exhausting, and dangerous. The rewards are very limited, short-term, and often costly to our natural environment (e.g., clear-cutting, some mining operations, landfill and ocean refuse disposal, noxious industries). Working with nature is often cheaper (once the technology is developed), less demanding, and safer. The rewards are greater (for more people), longer term, and environmentally neutral (e.g., solar energy) or positive (e.g., reforestation).

One of the greatest coalitions of energy forces in our natural environment is wildfire. As Australian Aboriginal people have always known, fire can be a great resource or a great risk. Historically, white Australians have ignored the risk of fire and hoped for the best, only to be forced to direct incredible human resources and effort into firefighting. Loss of life, crops, property, and resources have been considerable. Now, at last, we are being urged to learn simple but effective ways of living with fire risk instead of against it.

Similarly, one of the greatest energy forces in human nature is anger. As a potential emotional resource, anger has never been widely recognized. As a growing risk in our homes and workplaces and on our roads, anger is starting to attract significant public attention. By healing the pain that drives anger, we reduce the risks. By diverting residual anger energy into productive tasks, we capitalize on the resource value of anger.

Have you noticed the many similarities between anger and fire? Consider some of the linguistic expressions we use about anger: "hot under the collar"; "a burning rage"; "all fired up"; "cool it!"; "hose down the anger"; "sparked a public furor"; "he has a short fuse." There are dozens of these metaphors and euphemisms. Did you notice the expressions used by my clients in their PAMs in Part III? These are not just slips of the tongue, but are unconscious and cultural recognitions of the similarities between fire and anger. If we consider the basic principles of fire behavior, prevention, and suppression, we might uncover some really useful principles for reducing the risks associated with uncontrolled anger and diverting anger energy into positive outcomes.[4]

the power of fire

Recently, I joined the Country Fire Authority of Victoria as a volunteer firefighter. Mt. Macedon, where I live with my family, is one of the eight highest bushfire-risk areas in Victoria, so I figured the responsible thing to do was to join up and do my part. I'm so glad I did; as well as learning great team and individual skills for fighting fires, I have learned a lot about fire behavior I either never knew or took for granted. I am very much in awe of the mighty natural forces that are drawn together once a fire takes hold. I am sobered by the unimaginable damage, death, and injury that can be wrought by fire in so little time.

the fire triangle

I am especially impressed by more experienced firefighters and their enormous respect for the basic laws of nature that permeate their training and govern every strategic decision about the best way to go about approaching a particular fire. There could be no more devastating yet eloquent statement of natural law than that made by wildfire: You put energy in, you get energy out! The objective of firefighting (or more accurately, fire suppression) is to deny a fire one or more of its three energy inputs—fuel, heat, or air. They call it the "fire triangle"; break any one side and the fire cannot survive.

Heated fuel vaporizes; the vapor is ignited and burns; burning vapor heats more fuel, which in turn vaporizes; and so on. In the process, the fuel material breaks down as a result of the chemical process involved. Of course, the whole cycle will not start until ignition occurs. But when conditions are extreme—high temperature, high fuel load, dry air—ignition resistance is low.

I was astonished to discover the similarities in principle between fire behavior and anger behavior: between the coalition of energy forces around the fire triangle and those around the anger triangle, between the principles of natural law upon which fire-suppression strategy is developed and those upon which anger "suppression" strategy can be devised.

Most surprising of all were the many similarities in the characteristics and performance of fire fuel and those of anger fuel—an amazing metaphor.

fire fuel

Fire flourishes on old, decayed, dry, and warm fuel (e.g., dry grass, treefall, dense dried-out undergrowth), to which hot air has ready access. All it needs is ignition. If the ambient temperature is high, the atmosphere dry, and the air fanned by a good breeze, so much the better for fire. The fuel will heat to ignition point more quickly, will vaporize more readily, and will burn more intensely. Under extreme conditions of fuel, air, and heat, the fire will spread rapidly and, if unchecked, will race out of control. A wind change under these conditions converts a fast-moving, intense fire, burning on a narrow front and long flanks, into a raging inferno, as one of its flanks becomes a very wide and destructive front.

anger fuel

Anger flourishes on the volatile fuel of old, unhealed, and easily rekindled pain. If the interpersonal atmosphere is already tense, the surface fuel (recent or immediate pain, loss, fear, or perceived threat) will ignite readily. All that is needed is the heat of serious argument, emotional frustration, or even a physical injury (e.g., hitting the wrong nail with a hammer) to send the wildfire of anger on its path of destruction. If there is a "wind change" or assault from another direction (spouse or partner, the kids, the in-laws, the boss, the out-of-gas car, the nonstarting lawnmower), the focus of anger may suddenly rage on a much wider and more destructive front.

controlling fire and anger

The power of fire or anger burning out of control on a wide front is awesome indeed.

The behavior of fire and anger is similar because the properties of the energy forces that support them are similar. Similar also is the basic principle upon which are based effective strategies for risk reduction and suppression of both fire and anger—the reduction or elimination of one or more of the energy sources involved.

You can *suppress* or *control* fire a number of ways. By directing water at the seat of the fire, you can cool the fuel to a temperature that will not support vaporization, thus suppressing the fire by denying it heat energy. Alternatively, you can deny the fire its fuel energy, usually by mechanical or manual reduction or removal. Small fires can be smothered with earth or other nonflammable material through which air cannot travel. For major wildfires, however, smothering is not usually a viable option.

You can *reduce the risk* of fire—much the better option—by reducing or eliminating fuel loads. Ironically, much of this is done by controlled burning. You can enhance the wildfire protection rating of, for example, your family home by establishing a green belt of lawns and green growing plants. Replacing old, decayed, and dried-out fuel with new, vibrant, and well-nurtured growth is a great way to impede the progress of wildfire.

So, although the natural forces around a fire (wind, temperature, relative humidity, topography, etc.) are critical to strategic decision making, it is to the available fuel that the thrust of both prevention and suppression is directed.

And so it is with anger.

Prevention of risk of harm or damage from uncontrolled anger—*wildfire anger* if you like—is far superior (as an effective strategy) to anger *suppression*. Indeed, all that happens with suppression is that anger energy is redirected inwards to smolder away, much like a peat fire below the ground's surface. Anger-risk reduction, just like fire-risk reduction, is best achieved by the regular removal or reduction of fuel.

Every year around late spring, property owners around the Macedon ranges are encouraged by local government and fire authorities to clean up their land and buildings. If you drive around these parts any evening or weekend in October and November, you will see spirals of smoke dotting the hills and valleys, as residents burn trash, yard debris, dry grass, and fallen leaves. These ranges carry a very high fire-risk rating; big fires like those of Ash Wednesday, 1983, will explode through tree canopies as well as surface fuel in erratic and uncontrolled fury. Named for the day in 1983 with which most people associate the loss of many lives—including those of around eighteen fire-fighters—whole townships and settlements (including some in the Macedon ranges) burned to the ground. The "Ash Wednesday" wildfires in fact occurred over two weeks and raged across mountain ranges and lowlands from South Australia through Victoria to New South Wales. Some argue these were the greatest fires Australia has ever witnessed; most hope they never see anything like them ever again. Yet those same fires inspired bravery in the face of fear and recovery from devastation. So you can understand that the annual cleanup and burn-off is the most important fuel-reduction exercise around here.

anger is perennial

The problem with anger is we don't need a hot, dry summer to ignite the fuel. Wildfire is seasonal—but anger is perennial; it can flare up any time. In fact, winter is probably one of the worst seasons for anger, since we tend to be cooped up inside, head-to-head with each other. Therefore, to minimize the risk of harm or damage through anger, we need to engage in fuel removal or reduction as a regular part of our health regime. Just as a balanced diet and regular physical exercise reduce the rate at which excess fat is stored in the body, so a balanced emotional diet and regular expression of emotional energy reduce the rate at which negative energy is stored (under pressure) in the body. I should add here that physical exercise is also an effective instrument for expressing and releasing emotional energy.

reducing your emotional fuel

Obviously, one of the main ways of reducing the emotional fuel for anger is to express and heal the emotional pain that we men especially carry around with us. As I have said elsewhere, women carry pain, too, but they are generally much better at expressing and dealing with it than are we men. Please remember: Fuel reduction needs to be a regular activity. If you don't check your pain levels (fuel loading) regularly, you increase your risk of an anger episode.

You can see that as a volunteer firefighter, I am vitally interested in the theory and technology of all fire prevention and suppression techniques. But, as an anger specialist, I am fascinated by the metaphorical and technological support these techniques offer to those of us whose job it is to help people find ways of preventing serious episodes of anger and the attendant risks to life and property. If we can start to understand and appreciate anger as *energy*, having much in common with at least two of the energy forces around fire (fuel and heat), we will discover some new and exciting ways of working *with* our anger instead of *against* it.

Let us apply some fuel-reduction and heat-diversion principles to the energy of anger and see if we can produce some positive outcomes for ourselves, our families, and our communities. In the next and final chapter, we raise a few prospects for using anger in some surprisingly common and constructive ways.

putting your anger to good use

As you already know, anger energy can be powerful. Most probably, until you started this book, it has always come out in negative, destructive, or harmful ways. Yet, as you have just seen, anger energy can be used in positive ways, too. Some positive uses of anger can have outcomes on a national scale; others can change the lives of individuals, their families, or even the communities they live in.

turn anger energy into positive outcomes[1]

In your everyday life, there are many exciting and rewarding ways you can express or divert your anger energy. Best of all, you can do so in ways that satisfy your needs, values, and beliefs instead of conflicting with them.

turn your aros into a fitness program

One of the most serious health problems attached to our way of living these days (cars, TV, junk food, video games, etc.) is that most of us have become inactive. On the other hand, we are taking in more sugar and fat (energy) than ever before. Since anger is about energy, how much of our anger might be reduced if we either cut back the sugar and fat or worked it off? Look at your AROs, your lifestyle, and environment and see if any of the following ideas could work for you:

- Imagine those swimming pool laps you might have selected as an ARO becoming a daily routine.

- What about aerobics three times a week, or a fast walk for thirty minutes before breakfast?

- What about joining a gym? See a trainer and work your body.

- Maybe you could take up a sport or join your kids in theirs. Who knows, you could wind up coaching little league.

"Me fit???" you ask. Why not? Life as we know it could seriously change around here!

plan and implement a personal project

I am not talking about a game of pool over a beer at your local bar—where any energy you will express is far outweighed by the amount you are likely to ingest. I am talking about something that will seriously challenge your intellectual, emotional, and physical resources over a period of time, something that will not only divert your attention but will also divert your energy: something from which you will get an outcome of immense satisfaction, pride, and achievement.

- What about that self-improvement or hobby course you considered and never did anything about?

- Have you ever considered recreational music, theatre, or dance? You could get your partner or even the kids involved—a whole family project.

- Or, you could take up a craft—picture framing, pottery, woodwork.

- Or, how about an art—painting, drawing, poetry, sculpting, writing. Writing about your anger is a lot safer than acting it out.

get some useful tasks done

If you live in a house, what about those tasks around the place that have been waiting for months (or was it years?) to be done?

- The ground that needs turning over

- The trash to be loaded on a trailer

- The heavy stuff that nobody really wants to do

How much anger energy will those things absorb? How would you ever get them done without anger energy?

If you live in an apartment, what about doing something with the other residents? Get to know the neighbors instead of getting angry at them.

Or, there's the local school, church, or charity that just can't get enough volunteer labor for building, equipment, and grounds maintenance.

If you live in the city, what about exploring it—on foot (a great way to use up spare energy!). You could plan trips to different neighborhoods with your partner or the kids.

This is your life—get busy living it!

what about political action?

Yep! You can believe what you are reading: Politics at any level is, potentially, a tremendous avenue for expressing anger energy. And, you don't have to be a politician!

Senators, representatives, state legislators, mayors, city councilors, etc., are only some of the people who are active in politics. And their activities are only a few of the available ways to get involved in politics.

- What are the issues that make you mad?

- What would you do about them, if you could?

- Are there other people around you who feel the same?

- What about joining a political party, labor union, or other forum where you can press for change or just air your views?

get involved in a local action group

Consider some of the local community, social, environmental, or industrial action groups around your home or work. Used responsibly, some of these groups might value the input of your energy—anger energy or otherwise. (The church group to which my client Terry was attached was one of those.)

make your anger work *for* you

As you can see from the ideas above, the process of diverting (or channeling) anger energy is available to anyone and can take some surprising forms. To use this process requires only that you decide to act upon any issue around you that generates some sense of outrage in you. Read your local or state newspaper, your children's school newsletter, your work-place bulletin board—and decide to get involved.

Let us say your child's school is already stretched for funds and is about to be hit with another cutback that will jeopardize the education program. The school board is seeking support from parents for a letter-writing campaign or a delegation to your state legislator. You might offer your services to one of these activities, or even run for school board yourself!

Perhaps there is a story in your local paper about a development that will threaten the integrity of a major conservation estate (national park, waterway, old-growth forest, etc.). You never get involved in those things, but this one has your attention and outrage. You might decide to join the local protest movement and divert your anger energy into the issue.

Remember our discussions in Chapters 2 through 6 about anger as an expression of pain, especially the pain associated with some perceived assault upon the self. We also talked about the pain of alienation, the experience of feeling cut off from the processes of decision making that affect our lives. Getting involved in political and social action not only helps us to divert anger energy, it also helps to counter the alienation process by putting us back in touch with decision making in very active ways.

Like the energy of fire, the energy of anger is powerful, indeed. And, as with fire, we need to learn to live with anger instead of fighting against it. By owning and expressing our pain, instead of suppressing it, we reduce the fuel load of our anger. By diverting anger energy into activities that can produce positive outcomes, we get our anger to work for us instead of against us.

And, more importantly than any of that, we get to fulfil the mission we set out on at the very start of this book: We guarantee the safety and well-being of the women and children in our lives. If we men can do simply that, we will contribute much to the biggest issue of all—a world free of violence, a world at peace.

A pipe dream? Maybe. But remember this: Peace is like charity—it begins at home!

guidelines for practitioners

This is a brief guideline only. It is not a substitute for formal training courses conducted by *The Anger Clinic*. Information about these and other more comprehensive resources for practitioners are available from: www.angerclinic.com.au or www.hunterhouse.com.

a "thumbnail" theory of
dealing with your anger

As boys grow up, they learn to navigate their way to manhood with maps of masculinity, revealed by socialization and cultural influence. Men learn early to keep their pain and fear inside, safe from exposure and betrayal. It is in this sense that we can speak of some men becoming *alienated* from their (full) emotional lives, of being *"alienated from their emotional biography."* *Anger* becomes the culturally acceptable vehicle for their expression of pain and fear: Anger-driven violence is a product of their emotional alienation.

To reduce the incidence of male violence—interpersonal, family, or community—we need to understand and develop effective responses to the emotional alienation of angry and violent men. Critical sociology shows us how levels of alienation in a society are economically, structurally, and culturally produced. But, by definition, *emotional* alienation is experienced—or *not* experienced—by individuals in isolation.

When you reconnect a man with his emotional biography through the "window" of his anger, he can access, reintegrate, express, and resolve previously repressed or denied emotional experience. Men then become liberated from their emotional "anger drivers," pain and fear. Practical strategies are learned for directing and controlling anger and eliminating the risks of anger-driven violence.

Dealing with Your Anger bridges the gap between the social world and the emotional world, in which anger and violence are cogenerated: It links the personal and the political. *Dealing with Your Anger* is a biographical systems model of social, emotional, and cognitive reintegration. Because *Dealing with Your Anger* implicitly challenges dominant cultures of masculinity, power, and gender relations, it can support any current male family violence prevention program. See the Notes section starting on page 233 for additional discussions of theory and practice.

who is this guideline for?

This guideline is intended for counseling and psychotherapy practitioners from professional disciplines, such as social work, psychiatry, psychology, occupational therapy, pastoral care, rehabilitation, etc. It should assist practitioners in private practices, agencies, clinics, and programs. It will be especially useful to practitioners involved in the following:

- male family violence prevention programs and groups

- mental health clinics

- health and welfare agencies

- corrective services, including prison, probation, and parole

- justice systems and court diversion programs

- military services

- veterans services

- employee assistance programs

- men's health programs, etc.

what can you do with it?

Dealing with Your Anger was written primarily as a self-help book for men. With this assistive guideline, practitioners can use the book to support a *brief* and *fixed-session* counseling program for *individual* men who need to control their anger and stop their reactive violence. It is recommended you structure your program with clients around the chapters of *Dealing with Your Anger*, in the sessional format suggested below.

Although this *assistive guideline is not recommended* as a program for group work with men, *Dealing with Your Anger* is highly recommended as a set text for men's groups. At the time of writing, assistive guidelines for group work were being developed for inclusion in the professional support package mentioned above. Until they are completed, experienced practitioners should use their professional discretion about how best to apply the different strategies for change, especially those in Chapters 5 and 6. Less experienced practitioners should seek opportunities to work as cotherapists to colleagues experienced in group work.

CAUTION: In relationships where battering is actually or potentially an issue, all practitioners are asked to promote the primary principal of protection and safety of female partners and children. It is therefore highly recommended that the material in Chapter 1 be covered exhaustively—even if that means dedicating *all* of the first one or two sessions with your clients to it. Before starting in on the anger work of subsequent chapters, practitioners should have made a confident assessment that measures have been implemented to guarantee the safety and protection of partners and children. If in doubt, check your agency's protocols and policies or seek advice from the staff of a recognized family violence prevention program.

dealing with your anger:
a sessional format for counseling men

session	chapter(s)	content
session 1	**preamble & chapter 1**	Complete your usual intake, including presenting problems.
		Safety issues: Use "Men's Safety Check" at page viii and "What you should do now" at page vii.
		Outline how you plan to work through this book with your client, going through the Contents on pages v and vi.
		Explain your agency's policies and evaluation procedures.
		Offer real hope for positive change and your committed support to help make it happen.
		Using Chapter 1, raise the issues of anger, attitude, and violence.
		Homework: Client reads Chapter 1 and completes exercises.
session 2	**chapter 1**	Ask about the safety measures your client has adopted to protect his partner and children.
		Review and discuss the issues and exercises in Chapter 1, making sure you are clear about whether you are dealing primarily with an anger problem or an attitude problem.
		Consider again the safety measures against t the risk assessment you made in your joint review of Chapter 1.
		Complete your assessment and decide
		to proceed with anger work using this book,
		to refer your client to a batterers' or other program, or
		to do both.
		If you opt to proceed with anger work using this book or to do both, go ahead and schedule appointments for the rest of the program. Allow at least 1½ hours each for session 4 (Chapter 5) and session 5 (Chapter 6).
		Homework: Client reads Chapters 2 and 3.

dealing with your anger:
a sessional format for counseling men

session	chapter(s)	content
session 3	chapters 2 and 3	Review and discuss Chapters 2 and 3. Homework: Client reads Chapter 4 two or three times, then attempts *Emotional BioScan for Anger.*
session 4	chapter 5	Help client complete his *Emotional BioScan for Anger.* Your primary objective is to help your client identify his emotional anger drivers and the core issues of pain and fear that fuel them. You will need time, patience, and the willingness to explore and share your client's struggle with "new" emotional experience. *Without training, the best way to help your client do his BioScan is to experience doing your own BioScan first.*
		Homework: Client reads Chapter 6 thoroughly and attempts defuelling tasks, using the 'step 7' issues from his BioScan.
session 5	chapter 6	Review with your client his attempts to defuel his anger. Using the material from Chapter 6, use your own counseling or psychotherapy skills to help your client resolve the issues of pain and fear that, until now, have been driving his anger.
		Homework: Client takes a break and then reads Chapter 7.
session 6	chapter 7	Help your client identify an *off button,* a *difference maker,* and a *risk taker* that he can use in his life to avoid feeling angry.
		Homework: Client reads Chapter 8 and considers possible *Anger Release Options* in his immediate environment.
session 7	chapter 8	Help your client build a raft of *Anger Release Options*, making sure they are realistic, affordable, and energy exhausting.
		Homework: Client reads Chapters 9, 10, and 11.

dealing with your anger:
a sessional format for counseling men

session	chapter(s)	content
session 8	chapters 9, 10, & 11	Using the procedure described in Chapter 10, lead your client through the task of identifying all of his *anger signals*, regardless of the order or level of anger in which they occur.
		Using the traffic-light model and the processes described in Chapter 11, help your client to identify the different *anger levels* at which his signals occur—his log of *progressive anger signals*. There might be new signals or there might be a change in intensity or frequency of the same signals.
		Homework: Client reads Chapters 12 and 13.
session 9	chapters 12 and 13	Review and discuss the strategic choices available to your client at each level of his anger.
		Help your client to complete his *Personal Anger Monitor* and insert his signals in the appropriate boxes.
		Homework: Client practices his *Personal Anger Monitor* and reads Chapters 14 and 15.
session 10	chapters 5 & 6, 12 & 13, 14 & 15	Review *Emotional BioScan for Anger* and defuelling tasks.
		Review *Strategic Choices* and *Personal Anger Monitor*.
		Discuss similarities of fire and anger and consider effects in your client's personal, family, and work relationships.
		Canvas opportunities for putting anger energy to good use in your client's life.
		Schedule evaluation reviews for client and partner (joint or separate) in line with your own agency or practice policies.

notes

chapter one

1. Crowell, Nancy A., and Ann W. Burgess, eds., *Understanding Violence Against Women*, Washington, DC: National Academy Press, 1996.

2. National Crime Prevention, *Ending Domestic Violence? Programs For Perpetrators*, report to National Crime Prevention, Attorney General's Department, Canberra, 1999.

3. Pellegrini, Frank, "The McVeigh Trial," <www.Time.com>, 4 March 2001.

4. O'Brien, Bill, *Agents of Mayhem: The Global Phenomenon of Mass Murder*, Melbourne: Lothian, 2000.

5. The following works are of particular help in understanding the subtle and more obvious issues at work here:

   Brod, H., and Michael Kaufman, *Theorizing Masculinities*, Thousand Oaks, CA: Sage Publications, 1994, pp. 142–57.

   Hearn, Jeff, *The Violences of Men*, London: Sage Publications, 1998.

   Jackson, David, *Unmasking Masculinity*, London: Unwin Hyman, 1990.

6. Gilligan, James, *Violence: Our Deadly Epidemic and Its Causes*, New York: Putnam and Sons, 1996.

7. Ibid., cover.

8. Ibid., p. 213.

9. Ibid., p. 237.

10. O'Brien, op. cit., pp. 285–93.

11. "Murder-Suicides Follow Familiar Pattern," *The West Australian* (Perth), 12 January 1994.

12. Ibid.

13. Ibid.

14. The names and other material circumstances of all the men who appear in this book have been changed to protect their privacy. In most cases they have read and approved the text for publication. In a few cases contact has been lost and/or their whereabouts are now unknown.

chapter two

1. Burns, Robert, "Man Was Made to Mourn," orig. pub. 1786.

2. Threaten a man and he is most likely to get angry, so that you can't see his fear. In history, that response has saved the lives of whole

communities under attack. Today, it is not so useful. Hurt a man and he is most likely to get angry before he admits to hurting.

3. See Goleman, D., *Emotional Intelligence*, London: Bloomsbury, 1996, especially Part I, pp. 3–13, and Appendices A, B, C, and F.

4. McMillan, P., *Men, Sex and Other Secrets*, Melbourne: Text Publishing Company, 1992, extracts from pp. 42–44.

5. This concept comes from a school of sociology called symbolic interactionism. The Marx-inspired critical sociology, made possible by the post-Vietnam collapse of academic censorship and conservative scholarship, replaced the interactionists in academic popularity. Still, there was much of value that, in my work at least, has reemerged. The interactionist concept of the "social construction of self" played a major role in the development of Anger Therapy.

Specifically, the "self" that emerges from socialized childhood and adolescence into the gendered "self" of adulthood is the product of some ongoing negotiation between that person and the demands and expectations of her/his social world. To meet that person's need for approval and acceptance, and to avoid the painful sanctions of rejection, disapproval, threat, and/or punishment, the integrated wholeness of the infant is negotiated away into the gendered half-person of the adult. For men, this usually means surrendering the so-called "feminine" features of their humanity, including the ownership and expression of "unmanly emotions" like pain and fear. That series of "social learning" experiences we go through—by which, through our socialization, we become less than who we are—is what alienates us from the fullness of our selves. These experiences of socialization—whether they seem positive and rewarding at the time, or negative and punishing—are largely "done to us," since, as children, our share of social power to negotiate, question, or resist is nil or seriously limited. As adolescents struggling for our identity, our social power is not much greater. And as adults we tend to say "What the hell?" and just fit in or conform.

I call those "done to us" experiences of socialization—the ones that help to produce a self that is less than whole—"assaults upon our selfhood" or "assaults upon the self." They are the ones that evoke our pain, fear, and anger. As men, we mostly learn to own and express our anger, more so than the other emotions. Then our anger becomes our vehicle for expressing those other, "unmanly," emotions.

The most enduring interactionist studies of the social construction of self were those conducted in the 1950s and 1960s by Erving Goffman. He researched a number of closed institutions, including psychiatric hospitals, prisons, and elements of the military services and reported how "selves" were deconstructed (by a process he called "mortification of the self") and then reconstructed through a number of identifiable stages that the inmate negotiated. See Goffman, E., *Asylums*, New York: Anchor Books, 1961.

The crucial element that critical sociology added to Goffman's studies was an analysis that finally enabled us to see how closed institutions were the creation and reflection of their host society. Now we could see how the dominant interests, values, and related conflicts, which revolved around the economic base, social superstructure, and culture of a society, were the driving forces that created our closed institutions (prisons, nursing homes, military units, etc.). Critical sociology has also been able to show how the same interests, values, and conflicts are at work in shaping the structure and culture of our open institutions, like education, the law, government, religion, sports, entertainment, and the family.

The open institution equivalent of Goffman's "mortification of the self" is the socialization practice of assaults upon the self.

It is only on top of the normal processes of socialization that we then need to consider the additional impacts of any extraordinary trauma, e.g., physical or sexual abuse, emotional violence, violent modeling, etc. In short, it is not only the abused boy from a violent childhood who later develops a problem with anger; the normally socialized may well be angry also. In fact, childhoods where obvious violence or abuse were factors account for only 30 percent of all my clients.

The conclusion to which I am tempted is that reproducing masculinities by socialization is a serious assault upon the self, which reproduces anger and violence in men.

6. This is best understood by reference to the critical sociology of alienation. See, for example, Tönnies, F., *Community and Association (Gemeinschaft und Gesellschaft)*, trans. by Charles P. Loomis, London: Routledge and Kegan Paul, 1974; and Pappenheim, F., *The Alienation of Modern Man*, London and New York: Monthly Review Press, 1968. (Granted, you will need librarian assistance to unearth either of these once famous, now sadly overlooked, titles.) All I have done here is to take the sociology of alienation and extend it to the internal experience of the individual. (I find the term *internal* far more useful and specific than the term *subjective*.) Over two decades ago, Ely Zaretsky, one of the earliest profeminist writers and activists, applied this underused sociology to his analysis of the so-called nuclear family in Western society. See Zaretsky, E., *Capitalism, the Family and Personal Life*, London: Pluto Press, 1976.

7. This is the self that includes all those parts I hope nobody else can see or know, as much as it includes all those parts that I show of "me" to the outside. Ideally the "I" of me would be congruent with the "me." That is where sociology meets psychology, where interactionist meets psychotherapist. See Mead, G. H., *Mind, Self and Society*, ed. by C. Morris, Chicago: University of Chicago Press, 1934; and Rogers, Carl, *On Becoming a Person: A Therapist's View of Psychotherapy*, London: Constable, 1961.

8. Rogers, Carl, *On Becoming a Person*, p. 108.

9. The term *social image* is a more specific way of describing the "me" of self—the image of ourselves that we hope to present to the world and for which we will receive confirmation and acceptance, but not necessarily approval or reward from all quarters. Notice how some entertainers, notably in the genre of rock music, present images of violence, aggression, and indifference for which they are roundly condemned by the "guardians of moral values." See also Bob Connell's discussion of different masculinities presented as social images of self, but condemned by presenters of other, divergent masculinities. In Connell, R. W., *Masculinities*, Sydney: Allen and Unwin, 1995. See especially Chapters 4–7 in Part

II, "Four Studies of the Dynamics of Masculinity." As you read his text and the extracts from his interview transcripts, you come to know the concrete difference between the (social) self images of the interviewed men and their partly silenced whole selves—their "I" of "me."

10. For a comprehensive presentation of this dynamic, see Lerner, H. G., *The Dance of Anger*, New York: Harper and Row, 1985.

chapter three

1. Blake, William, "A Poison Tree," in *Songs of Experience*, orig. pub. 1794.

2. This is the most controversial element in most contemporary debates about male family violence. Cognitive psychology—including its principal applications in Cognitive Behavioral Therapy (CBT) and Rational Emotive Therapy (RET)—variously seeks to train the intellect, or rational brain, of the client to take control over anger impulses. Even narrative therapy—a more empowering and effective approach—depends heavily upon cognitive restorying, i.e., striving with the client as he learns to reauthor his essentially emotional experience of life.

Pure profeminist approaches simply assert that, since anger is a chosen emotion, its use is really another manifestation of dominant male power and control. This argument is often supported with examples of what might be called "anger discrimination" or "selective anger," e.g., "If someone knocked on the door when I was arguing with my wife, I could stop midsentence—I would instantly become Mr. Nice Guy. The second they left it was like turning a tape recorder back on—I could start exactly where I left off" (George). In McLellan, Gordon, "Mad or Bad? You're More in Control Than You Think," Chapter 8, pages 61–66, in Frances, R., ed., *Mirrors, Windows and Doors*, orig. pub. 1994, rev. by N. Belfrage and I. Wilson, Melbourne: V-NET, 1998.

This argument overlooks the dynamically interactive nature of anger in interpersonal relations. Certainly at the peaks of rage, accounts abound of barroom brawls where a man takes on anybody in the heat of battle, so to speak. But this is not the norm in family violence—unless someone attempts to intervene in a conflict that is already out of hand (another way of saying out of control). It is with my wife that I may have lost it, not with the next-door neighbor or the police.

This is not to say that anger is never used consciously, nor that violence is never strategic—that would be absurd. Equally absurd, or at least unhelpful, is to persist rigidly with our professional adherence to cognitive, intellectual (sometimes ideological) paradigms, when we really need to engage experiential, emotional paradigms.

Just as we professionals first are required to know and develop our intellectual skills in university programs, before we are let loose on clients, so should we be required to know and develop our emotional skills. This is long overdue in the disciplines that graduate people into the so-called helping professions. It is vital for professionals who deal with people who have problems in any of the emotional areas. But nowhere is this emotional education so important as it is for those professionals who would deal with anger and violence.

3. This is a major departure from cognitive theory, and a radical addition to feminist theory. Both schools—and they are not necessarily exclusive — emphasize choice. The feminist school extends that notion to power and control. And that is the trap sprung by overdependence upon rational thinking. In fact, the experience of anger and/or violence is quite obviously and drastically different for the person who is delivering the anger and/or violence than it is for the person receiving it. Even to state that is to oversimplify the escalation produced in dynamic interaction between two or more people. (For the experience of women around anger, see Lerner, H. G., *The Dance of Anger.*)

   The error in the "male power and control" argument seems to come about this way: When women report the crushing experience of feeling disempowered and controlled by a man's anger, we take that experience and assign it as the intent, motive, or "project" of the man. We make a leap of logic that goes, "If I experience a man's behavior in this certain way, then his behavior is designed to make me experience it that way." Now, of course, that may well hold up where the woman's experience is learned by the man, who in turn uses that behavior— regardless of his emotional state—strategically to impose power and control. But in my own experience of this work, men use anger as "strategy" in a minority of cases, not in the majority.

   Abused, violated, and even physically injured by a man's violence, women don't routinely differentiate between his anger-reactive violence and his strategic violence. And there is, to date, no evidence that their experience of violence is any different, one way or the other. From the victim's point of view, there is no difference.

   The evidence for that claim lies in the successful outcomes obtained (84 percent) in the face-to-face work upon which this book is based. Whether self-help via this book is as effective as "live" work remains to be seen. The point is that if power and control were always the objective of a man's anger, the results of the work that I and others do with angry men, at the level of emotional experience, would be zero. The contributor to the success of this work is our willingness—client and therapist—to work with emotional experience. To do so necessitates our accepting that anger is not necessarily about control, but is more often about losing control. That is not to deny that anger can be and is used as a controlling force—as violence—in many situations.

4. This notion of self-restoration or reintegration will occur frequently throughout the book, but especially here and in Part II. It is the most obvious response to the problem of alienation discussed above. So far as I know, the sociology of alienation has never before been applied to the practice of psychotherapy with angry and violent men. I am here to tell you, it is a very powerful and empowering application.

5. To me, it made more sense to resolve the emotional drivers of Rajid's anger and violence than it did to stop his violence. Where juvenile corrective institutions and adult prisons had failed, who was I to try? You will read later how emotional restoration and resolution not only succeeded in reducing Rajid's anger-reactive violence, but also led him to question and change his values, occupation, and lifestyle.

6. Certainly childhood trauma has a big impact upon our emotional development, but so too does our routine socialization into whatever "masculinities" are dominant in our particular milieu. That point is well illustrated in Patrick's story, where divisions of labor and responsibility, ideas about control (men over business and work; women over home, emotions, and values), and so on dominated the landscape as Patrick became more like his dad in every way.

chapter four

1. Moore, George, *The Brook Kerith*, orig. pub. 1916.

2. Most of us understand that we have a biography, a personal history of our life, that could be written or taped for others to read or hear. We could break down that biography into parts: physical, occupational, social, intellectual, spiritual, etc. Although each part is inseparable from the whole life, it is as though they also exist separately on their own tracks, or in their own stories within a story.

   Our health and fitness, careers, social life, marriage, family, education and training, church or religion, intellectual development, and so on each have their own stories. Although they all are parts of the whole, they can be spoken of and written of separately. In this way, we can understand our emotional biography, the path that contains our emotional experiences. This is important because if we can accept and understand the idea of an emotional biography, then, as with any biography, we can write about it. In Chapter 5, you will see the importance of doing so.

3. Biddulph, S., *Manhood: An Action Plan for Changing Men's Lives*, Sydney: Finch Publishing, 1995.

chapter five

1. Roman philosopher Seneca, quoted in Hayward, S., and M. Cohan, *Bag of Jewels*, Avalon: In-Tune Books, 1999.

2. This is an exciting development that has taken several years to emerge out of my various practice settings. It is a very effective instrument for making emotional experience accessible and acceptable to men and available for owning and reintegrating into their conscious lives. But the BioScan also provides a unique cognitive reframe. Anger—originally the stuff of guilt, remorse, harm, and damage—becomes instead the instrument or pathway to emotional reintegration. For men, this process seems to provide an immediate boost to self-esteem and clinches a commitment to work for positive change.

3. This task demands a significant commitment of time, effort, and energy. So when men start to write their BioScan—and when they complete the task—they seem to become totally committed to the process of change.

chapter six

1. Peck, M. Scott, M.D., *The Road Less Traveled*, London: Hutchinson, 1978, p. 15.

2. This comes from the earlier work of Richard Bandler and John Grinder, who adapted the system of transformational grammar to the practice of psychotherapy. (See Bandler, R., and J. Grinder, *The Structure of Magic*, Palo Alto, CA: Science and Behavior Books, vol. 1, 1975; vol. 2, 1976.) It was this work that subsequently formed the communication base of the better-known and highly popular Neuro Linguistic Programming (NLP). (See Bandler and Grinder, *Frogs into Princes*, Moab, UT: Real People Press, 1979, and *ReFraming*, Moab, UT: Real People Press, 1982.)

   Their theoretical bottom line is this: To understand human behavior and interaction, we need to understand the way we use language to model and represent our experience of ourselves in our world.

   Where language is superficial, incomplete, or diminished, we make, transmit, and receive superficial, incomplete, and diminished representations or accounts (stories) of our experience. One way this happens in our culture is through our increasing trend to convert (linguistically) our doings, feelings, thinkings, experiencings, and interactings into simple objects or items with names. Grammatically speaking, we translate our verbs into nouns. A hurt or injury, for example, does not need a subject or object to be articulated; it can seem to stand alone. "Am hurt" or "was injured," by contrast, will not stand alone; at the very least, these phrases require subjects, and usually objects. So a full representation of "hurt" might be "I feel hurt when you say those things to me."

   I've found that by encouraging clients to use full linguistic representations for their emotional experiences, they become better able and more willing to recognize and own them for themselves, and less likely to deny or disown them.

3. Biddulph, S., *Manhood: An Action Plan for Changing Men's Lives*, Sydney: Finch Publishing, 1995, p. 209.

4. Ibid., p. 186.

5. Ibid., p. 208.

chapter seven

1. The beliefs that we often have about the external causes of our anger have been challenged since 1957, when Albert Ellis first presented his ABC's of Rational Emotive Therapy (RET). For a summary of the history and practice of RET specifically, and the cognitive therapies generally, see Chapters 8 and 9 in Bonger, B., and L. Beutler, eds., *Comprehensive Textbook of Psychotherapy: Theory and Practice*, Oxford: Oxford University Press, 1995. Similar ideas about subjective interpretation of external events as anger arousers are canvassed in the literature dealing with Social Information Processing. What is being suggested here, however, should not be confused with the theories of these schools.

Here we are promoting acts of emotional courage rather than acts of rational or cognitive insight. Different responses to the same anger stimuli—however significant or trivial—can break the vicious cycle of anger. If a man can break that cycle at routine levels of anger, he is well placed to prevent the escalation of mood that is so typical of a rising anger cycle. The stories of "The Off Button" and "The Difference Maker" that follow illustrate this simple dynamic. The third story in the sequence, "The Risk Taker," is a little deeper but implements similar principles of prevention.

2. See previous note.

chapter eight

1. By this I mean the metaphor that quite elegantly describes the internal experience of "dynamic thrust" reported by so many men. The cybernetic systems work of Gregory Bateson (1973, 1980, see reference below) has much to offer the question "What makes some men explode with rage?" by asking instead "What prevents or restrains some men in some circumstances from so exploding?" In the metaphorical sense, all emotion is energy, so when men or women suppress their emotions, they restrain an energized part of their self-experience.

When a woman is feeling guilty and depressed, we need to ask, "What emotional part of herself is she suppressing or restraining?" The answer so often is her anger, to which she may be socialized in our culture to feel unentitled. How long ago was it that when a woman did express anger, she was regarded and even diagnosed as hysterical?

When a man is seriously angry—out of proportion perhaps to the triggering event—we need to ask, "What other emotional part of himself is being expressed here, and what has been restrained?" The answer most often is his fear and/or pain.

Not so popular today as in the 1970s and 1980s, cybernetic systems theory is still a useful aid to understanding emotions like anger, and their associated behaviors. (See Bateson, G., *Steps to an Ecology of Mind*, London: Paladin, 1973, and *Mind and Nature: A Necessary Unity*, Isle of Man: Fontana, 1980.)

2. This a more understandable way of talking about the effects of chemical stimulants on the central nervous system. This, of course, implicates the amygdala (now understood as an emotional switchboard) and the entire limbic system, as much as it does the neocortical brain. See Goleman, D., *Emotional Intelligence*.

chapter nine

1. O'Casey, Sean, *The Plough and the Stars*, act 2, orig. pub. 1926.

2. Many professionals and academics will throw up their hands in horror at this apparent statement of emotional determinism. They will point to the empirical and ideological evidence that says "anger is chosen" and that men can control it if they choose to. And that may well be so—at

the rational level. The problem is that anger is emotional, and most experience it that way. Therefore, if you do no more than simply confront him with his "choice" to be angry, you alienate him even further from the emotional drivers of his anger, from his selfhood, and indeed from you.

So, I start from where the client is, instead of from where the theory and ideology are. I'll be able to get back to the latter as soon as I need them. Given that one of the worst fears for men is of being out of control, when you accept that a man can experience his extreme level of anger as "being out of control," you actually can win his commitment to doing something about it. That's what this is all about: getting men to take responsibility, not only for their violent behavior, but for the emotions that drive it.

This is a good place to raise a question with my peers. It has bothered me for 26 years, ever since I worked with the dispossessed, marginalized, and impoverished Aboriginal people of Australia's northwest. They were angry—very angry—at their experience of white Australia for over 150 years. My question is this: How come we charge the frustrated, the "assaulted," the wounded with choosing their anger, but we do not charge the bereaved with choosing their grief, nor the betrayed with choosing their hurt, nor the terrorized with choosing their fear?

It is pointless commanding anyone to control his or her emotions without the tools to do so—unless you can reverse the experience that has triggered the emotion. So what we need to do with men who have serious problems with anger is to lead them to their own tools for controlling it. That's what these Chapters in Part III set out to do.

3. I have said elsewhere that anger therapy—via this self-help book or face-to-face with a therapist—will not directly solve the problem of strategic (as opposed to anger-reactive) violence. And that seems to be true. But there seems to develop an astonishing ancillary of anger therapy with clients who have owned the practice of strategic violence at home, at work, or in their social life. Rajid, and other similar men, began to question his whole value system and the violent lifestyle those values supported. And he made conscious decisions to change. For me, this has been one of the most exciting outcomes of the work so far. If that ancillary pattern holds up under research conditions, the potential implications for policy and service delivery are enormous.

4. To deal effectively with anger, I believe we need to develop strategies and programs for both the emotional and the behavioral elements. I further believe that such programs must be integrated, if they are to effectively promote men's reintegration and effectively counter the alienation process. I guess it's more than just "the right tool for the right job"; it's really about having all the tools needed to complete the job.

chapter ten

1. Practitioners familiar with CBT (Cognitive Behavioral Therapy) and NLP (Neuro Linguistic Programming) will recognize the simple cognitive reframe that's been done here with Rajid. The same is done with all of

my anger clients; I have taken as many elements as I can access of a man's experience with serious anger and made them conscious and "live." Later I "anchor" them (in NLP terms) to work as signals in his personal anger monitor, or PAM.

2. Physical cues, like tremors or shaking, tend to intensify body tension, impelling us towards tension release, weakening our emotional controls, and propelling anger upwards. As the pace and volume of heartbeat increases, the sense of dizziness some people experience works again to "fuel" the emotional experience of escalating anger, which in turn further accelerates heartbeat, and so the cycle continues. It seems to be this autonomic feedback effect that has so much to do with the experience of losing control at the higher "threshold" levels of anger.

   The autonomic feedback effect will be familiar to CBT and NLP practitioners. It will also be central to the thinking of practitioners and academics schooled in the cybernetic systems framework. In fact, what I have really done to develop this system of anger control is to extend systems thinking from the social and interpersonal spheres into the internal life of the individual. To NLP, of course, nothing would have been more natural or logical. I've discussed the idea of anger as energy already; now we're concerned with the idea of communication—specifically internal communication about internal information. This idea makes use of the work of both Bandler and Grinder and Gregory Bateson. The autonomic feedback effect, reported by so many of my clients and colleagues, is one of the key features of rising anger.

chapter eleven

1. Roethke, Theodore, "The Exorcism," orig. pub. 1958.

2. Some men in therapy report the experience of climbing through the emotional scale of anger, to a point at which they seem to become calm, cold, calculating, and methodical. This occurs when they have gone way over their threshold, where they would otherwise be considered least likely to make conscious choices and least able to control their anger. I do not yet fully understand this feature. It is as though at their worst state of emotional disturbance, their "best" intellectual faculties come to the fore in the service of their rage. I'd appreciate any comments or insights about this phenomenon from colleagues working or researching in this field.

chapter twelve

1. Quoted in Hayward, S., and M. Cohan, *Bag of Jewels*.

2. As a social worker, sociologist, and psychotherapist, I have always felt frustrated by cognitive and behavioral approaches to anger management. Whether it was RET (Rational Emotive Therapy), CBT (Cognitive Behavioral Therapy), SIP (Social Information Processing), or behavior modification, the process always seemed to depend upon the client being able to conduct complex rational analyses, interpretations, and choices while in a state of rising emotional disturbance.

It seemed to me that we needed a set of choices that could be more easily made within an emotional experience. That meant "keep it simple," and use experiential information that is immediately recognizable and accessible, rather than intellectual information that seems (in the moment) unclear and remote. In this system, only one choice is to be made at any level, with the anger-escalation option always being one of them. That is both realistic and self-affirming.

3. For me, this is the most empowering cognitive reframe in this entire system of anger control; it takes the self-defeating blame stance, the moral accusation, even the "your responsibility" stance—which is implicit and obvious anyway—and turns it all into a question of expertise. This stance confirms the angry man as an acting human being with the integrity and ability to control his anger; and it does so with a salutation instead of condemnation. It is, in the end, the one thing that makes self-change possible at all.

chapter thirteen

1. Shakespeare, William, *King Lear*, act 1, scene 5, orig. pub. 1605–6.

2. The sorts of tasks PAM is asked to do for a man reflect the sorts of tasks men typically expect "their women" to do, thereby continuing their own self-alienation while subjecting their partners to unrealistic and unjust responsibilities. PAM is no more than a newly awakened part of the man himself. By learning the anger-control strategies presented in this book, men begin to take back their own responsibilities and freedoms. In the process, they relieve the burden imposed on their female partners.

chapter fourteen

1. Dewey, Karen, *Angry: Scarred for Life*, Sydney: Pan Macmillan (Ironbark), 1994, p. 239.

2. Biddulph, S., *Manhood*, p. 209.

3. Because of the specific meaning and pivotal role of energy in physics, it has been nigh impossible to relate the concept to behavior and emotions—at least in formal theory. By 1970, the attempts of Freud and his psychoanalysts, along with those of the early behavioral scientists, were profoundly dumped by Bateson and his cybernetic school: "energy is Mass Velocity^2," says Bateson (*Steps to an Ecology of Mind*, p. 28), and that's that! Yet every man (and woman) I have ever worked with or talked to about anger, one way or another, describes the chemical and neurological hyperactivity of anger in ways that suggest the rush and flow of energy.

   That in turn takes us to today's "ventilate versus suppress" argument. It is true that uncontrolled anger ventilation seems to habituate our anger and that chronic anger has been linked by several medical and medicopsychological studies to heart disease. On the other hand, it seems that anger suppression can reduce cardiac pumping efficiency and promote heart attack. See Goleman, D., *Emotional Intelligence*, especially Chapter 11, "Mind and Medicine," pp. 164–85. (While it may be convenient for some to write off Goleman's work itself as "pop psychology," the many seriously conducted, academically driven research studies quoted cannot so easily be dismissed.)

Since there is, as yet, no evidence of biological factors in this cardiac–anger link, but only chemical and neurological interactions and reactions, it seems to me we can now reconsider the role of energy in anger.

Again, ordinary men and women experience the energy of their anger. As long as working with anger as energy seems to work so well, I'm very happy to keep using it. And, if it does turn out to be just another cognitive reframe, so what? The concept of anger as energy gives a man a handle on his anger, which enables him to redirect it into useful purposes with positive outcomes. Like returning to him the status of being the best expert about his own anger, the energy paradigm is equally empowering; therefore, it generates change.

4. In my experience, men relate very well to fire. Men's captivation with fire and fire-related activities probably goes back to boyhood dreams about fire engines, flashing lights and sirens, daring rescues, and heroic firefighters. As adults, living in a country where fire is a serious annual threat that claims many lives and properties, men and women develop a healthy respect for the awesome power of wildfire.

Since there are so many metaphorical similarities between the energies, fuels, forces, and performances of fire and anger, it makes for a very practical and accessible way of exploring the potential for anger prevention. It also demonstrates the potential for diverting anger energy into positive outcomes.

Nonetheless, the fire metaphor for anger is just that—metaphor: I have found it a useful one.

chapter fifteen

1. One of the most paradoxical uses of fire in wildfire high-risk areas is the annual controlled burn-off of ground fuel; we literally prevent fire with fire. Men can use anger energy in a similar way. We can focus and use our anger energy to achieve, or take part in the pursuit of, worthwhile individual, family, or community objectives. By channeling our anger energy into positive outcomes, we can actually reduce the risk of damaging and destructive anger at home.

Again, NLP and CBT practitioners will recognize a dynamic reframe here. Once something to be hidden from public view in shame and guilt, anger now becomes an engine for a man's potential contributions to community life.

bibliography

Bandler, R., and J. Grinder, *The Structure of Magic*, Palo Alto, CA: Science and Behavior Books, vol. 1, 1975; vol. 2, 1976.

——, *Frogs into Princes*, Moab, UT: Real People Press, 1979.

——, *ReFraming*, Moab, UT: Real People Press, 1982.

Bateson, G., *Steps to an Ecology of Mind*, London: Paladin, 1973.

——, *Mind and Nature: A Necessary Unity*, Isle of Man: Fontana, 1980.

Biddulph, S., *Manhood: An Action Plan for Changing Men's Lives*, Sydney: Finch Publishing, 1995.

Bonger, B., and L. Beutler, eds., *Comprehensive Textbook of Psychotherapy: Theory and Practice*, Oxford: Oxford University Press, 1995.

Brod, H., and Michael Kaufman, *Theorizing Masculinities*, Thousand Oaks, CA: Sage Publications, 1994.

Connell, R. W., *Masculinities*, St. Leonards, Australia: Allen and Unwin, 1995.

Crowell, Nancy A., and Ann W. Burgess, eds., *Understanding Violence Against Women*, Washington, DC: National Academy Press, 1996.

Dewey, Karen, *Angry: Scarred for Life*, Sydney: Pan Macmillan (Ironbark), 1994.

Farrelly, F., and J. Brandsma, *Provocative Therapy*, Cupertino, CA: Meta Publications, 1974.

Frances, R., ed., *Mirrors, Windows and Doors*, orig. pub. 1994, rev. by N. Belfrage and I. Wilson, Melbourne: V-NET, 1998.

Gilligan, James, *Violence: Our Deadly Epidemic and Its Causes*, New York: Grosset/Putman, 1996.

Goffman, E., *Asylums*, New York: Anchor Books, 1961.

Goleman, D., *Emotional Intelligence*, London: Bloomsbury, 1991.

Hearn, Jeff, *The Violences of Men*, London: Sage Publications, 1998.

Jackson, David, *Unmasking Masculinity*, London: Unwin Hyman, 1990.

Lerner, H. G., *The Dance of Anger*, New York: Harper and Row, 1985.

McMillan, M., *Men, Sex and Other Secrets*, Melbourne: Text Publishing Company, 1992.

Mead, G. H., *Mind, Self and Society*, ed. by C. Morris, Chicago: University of Chicago Press, 1934.

"Murder-Suicides Follow Familiar Pattern," *The West Australian* (Perth), 12 January 1994.

National Crime Prevention, *Ending Domestic Violence? Programs for Perpetrators*, report to National Crime Prevention, Attorney General's Department, Canberra, 1999.

O'Brien, Bill, *Agents of Mayhem: The Global Phenomenon of Mass Murder*, Melbourne: Lothian, 2000.

Pappenheim, F., *The Alienation of Modern Man*, London and New York: Monthly Review Press, 1968.

Peck, M. Scott, M.D., *The Road Less Traveled*, London: Hutchinson, 1978.

Pellegrini, Frank, "The McVeigh Trial," <www.Time.com>, 4 March 2001.

Rogers, Carl, *On Becoming a Person: A Therapist's View of Psychotherapy*, London: Constable, 1961.

Tönnies, F., *Community and Association (Gemeinschaft und Gesellschaft)*, trans. by Charles P. Loomis, London: Routledge and Kegan Paul, 1974.

Zaretsky, E., *Capitalism, the Family and Personal Life*, London: Pluto Press, 1976.

index